The Complete Guide to World
MYSTICISM

TIMOTHY FREKE

& PETER GANDY

PIATKUS

This book is dedicated to
The One
I
Love

© 1997 Timothy Freke and Peter Gandy

First published in 1997 by
Judy Piatkus (Publishers) Ltd,
5 Windmill Street, London W1P 1HF

First paperback edition 1998

**The moral right of the author
has been asserted**

*A catalogue record for this book is available
from the British Library*

ISBN 0 7499 1682 6 (hb)
ISBN 0 7499 1776 8 (pb)

Cover design and illustration
by Gary Day-Ellison
Illustrated by Zena Flax

Data capture by Phoenix Photosetting, Chatham
Image capture by Selwood Systems, Midsomer Norton
Printed and bound in Great Britain by
Butler & Tanner Ltd, Frome and London

CONTENTS

◆

FOREWORD

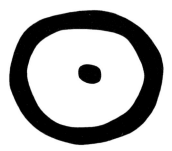

This modern astronomical symbol for the sun is also found on Egyptian pyramid texts dating from 2500 BC.

*T*HERE can be no final and definitive statement about anything. This book, like any other, is necessarily a personal and selective view of a profound and expansive subject. It is a product of an enthusiasm for mysticism which we have shared from our early teenage years. Growing up in a culture in which for the first time different spiritual traditions were readily accessible, we embraced the opportunity to explore world spirituality in a way that was simply not available to previous generations. Although we have often travelled separate paths, we have always come together to compare experiences, realizations and doubts; to encourage and challenge each other; and slowly to push back the frontiers of our understanding.

We were both brought up in the Christian tradition; however, from an early age we also sought out the insights of other faiths and philosophies. Between us we have received instruction from Buddhist masters in Thailand, Hindu gurus in India, Native American shamans, Tibetan lamas, Franciscan friars, Kabbalists, magicians and Sufi dancers. We have explored psychedelics, studied for university degrees in Western philosophy from the ancients to the present day, received spiritual initiations, made pilgrimages to sacred sites from Greece to Peru, practised yoga and fasting, made many spiritual retreats, and taught meditation and Tai Chi Chuan. Although committed to a particular path while exploring it, we have not become affiliated to any one tradition. We have constantly had to guard against the danger of superficiality, but the nature of the times and our own particular lives has led us to this wide variety of spiritual experience. This has, we feel, put us in an ideal position to write a book on world mysticism, presenting a genuine overview, unencumbered by the dogmas of any one tradition, yet with respect for all. We have been able to draw not only on academic research, but directly on our own personal encounters.

Our experiences have led us to an open-minded eclecticism which seeks the common factors within all mystical traditions. We have attempted to unearth the hidden history of mysticism that runs like a thread through all religions, but belongs to none of them. In our modern multicultural world, we hope our approach will be some small contribution to finding a spiritual basis for human unity, beyond partisan religious divisions. We have drawn on the very latest scholarly opinion, which often challenges the accepted view – consequently, much of the history in this book may be surprising. Limited space has made it impossible for us to justify all that we have said, but we hope it will at least provoke questions and reveal new possibilities. It will undoubtedly upset some who are deeply embedded within the viewpoint of one particular religious tradition, but our intention is not to criticize or confront – rather to build bridges to a common understanding of a common human spirituality.

Throughout our personal explorations of world spirituality, one thing has remained constant – the spontaneous arising of mystical experiences. We are certainly not saintly, wise or special in any way, and so are able to say with the authority of personal knowledge that such experiences are not the preserve of an exemplary few. They are natural human realizations open to all. We hope this book may challenge the elitist view that the direct experience of the Truth – whether called God, Tao, enlightenment or whatever – is available only to the piously religious or fanatically disciplined. There have been great mystics of many different types. Some have been saints and others rogues. Some have been religious and others mavericks. It is not a mystic's character that makes him or her a mystic, but the experience of a transcendental reality beyond the limits of personality. Mysticism is not some high tower accessible only to the chosen few, but the very essence of the human adventure.

Timothy Freke and Peter Gandy

INTRODUCTION

We shall not cease from exploration
And the end of all our exploring
Will be to arrive where we started
And know the place for the first time.

Quick, now, here, now, always –
A condition of complete simplicity
(Costing not less than everything).

T. S. ELIOT
Little Gidding

TOWARDS the end of his life the Swiss psychologist Carl Jung was interviewed on a television programme called 'Face to Face'. As a pupil of Freud, he had set out in his youth to scientifically explore the secrets of the mind, and had discovered the perennial mystical Truth witnessed by saints and visionaries of all times and all places. Now a grey-haired bespectacled old man, his eyes twinkling and his soul animated by the wisdom born of a lifetime's self-inquiry, he had become both scientist and sage. During the interview he was asked if he believed in God. With the complete conviction that comes from personal experience he replied 'I know that God exists. I don't need to believe, I *know*.'

Like Carl Jung, the great mystics of all spiritual traditions claim to have been transported beyond second-hand doctrines to certain experiential knowledge of the Truth. Mysticism is concerned with the possibility of personally encountering a spiritual reality which is hidden from our normal awareness like the sun behind the clouds. It is not concerned with propounding a philosophy that may be believed or doubted. The mystics tell us that higher consciousness is available to everyone, and by setting out on our own journey of spiritual exploration we can experience it for ourselves.

In this book you will find the inspiring words of some of these great souls who have explored this mystical experience. They share with us their understanding and delight. We are introduced to the world's saints and sages throughout history, who give us their personal testimony that the Truth is waiting to welcome all those who sincerely set out in search of it.

In Chapters 1–10 we meet the Shamanic mystics of the Native Americans, Australian Aborigines and ancient Indo-Europeans who underwent harrowing ritual death and ate powerful psychedelic plants to achieve ecstatic visions; Hindu mystics like Sai Baba the man of miracles and Sri Nisargadatta the enlightened tobacconist; zany Zen Buddhist masters who ridicule each other; Taoist sages who believe they do nothing; philosophers of the Mystery Schools - the spiritual universities of the ancient Greeks and Egyptians; Jewish mystics like the dancing Baal Shem; Christian mystics who found knowledge through ignorance and the early heretical Christians called Gnostics; Islamic mystics called Sufis who treated God as a lover; and mystics

This symbol shows how all religions spring from one source. The fountain is the source and the religions illustrated here are Hinduism, Buddhism, Islam, Christianity and the Parsees.

No one's mouth is big enough to utter the whole thing.

ALAN WATTS
Modern Mystic

It is better to see God in everything than to try and figure it out.

N E E M K A R O L I
B A B A
Modern Hindu mystic

who have flourished outside of any religious tradition, like the scientists who received their insight from angels. This plethora of great masters and different spiritual paths is only an outer veil covering the essential simplicity of the mystics' message which is examined in Chapter 11. Finally, in Chapter 12, we explore how to transform the lives we are already living into a journey of awakening. The mystics may help us to discover in the daily unfolding of our lives something so obvious it was overlooked – the Mystery of Life.

A W I S D O M B E Y O N D W O R D S

There is a Hindu teaching story about a king who asks a sage to explain mysticism. In response, the sage asks the king how he would convey the taste of a mango to someone who had never eaten anything sweet. No matter how hard the king tries, he cannot adequately describe the flavour of the fruit, and in frustration, he demands of the sage 'Tell me then, how would you describe it?'. The sage picks up a mango and hands it to the king saying 'This is very sweet. Try eating it!'.

The mystics know they can never fully explain mysticism to us, but by expressing their own joy and amazement, they may entice us into tasting the fruit for ourselves. Reading this book is an opportunity to catch the mystical vision. All mystics despair of ever being able to find the language to completely convey the wonder of their insights. Their enthusiasm, however, can be as infectious as laughter, gently leading us to a wisdom beyond words.

The 16th century Jewish mystic Isaac Luria wrote 'I can hardly open my mouth to speak without feeling as though the sea burst its dam and overflowed. How then shall I express what my soul has received?' Ultimately words are inadequate to express the immediacy of the mystical vision. As Zen Master Daie said, 'All the teachings the sages expounded in the sacred scriptures are no more than commentaries on the sudden cry – Ah, this!'.

Although the mystics are forced to use words to communicate, they really want to bring our attention to the silence within which words are spoken. The Hindu sage Ramana Maharshi would sit without speaking for hours with his disciples, giving what he called 'silent teachings', which he regarded as his highest revelations. There is a fable that when Buddhist missionaries first took the teachings of the Buddha to China, they were appalled to find they had taken books full of blank pages. Returning to India, they asked the Buddha what this meant. The Buddha insisted that these were his genuine teachings, but if they could not be understood, he would reluctantly consent to speak words. As the Native American mystic Black Elk puts it, 'Is not silence the very voice of Great Spirit?'

A NATURAL STATE OF KNOWING

The ideas of the mystics contained within this book are like the word 'silence' which breaks the silence in order to bring our attention to it. The mystics use the beauty of ideas to inspire a vision of a spiritual reality that outstrips intellectual understanding. Concepts and ideas may form a bridge to this understanding, but he who remains on the bridge never reaches his destination. The Zen masters compare their teachings to a finger pointing at the moon – the finger is not the moon and anyone who remains fixated with the finger will have missed the point. Mystical knowledge is like knowing a country because you have been there, compared to which mere mental 'knowledge' is like only having seen a map or read a travelogue. With such opinions someone may *appear* wise but will not *be* wise. The message of the mystics is that just as saying the word 'medicine' will not cure an illness of the body, so theories and beliefs cannot heal the sickness of the soul. If we wish to relieve our bodily hunger we must eat the meal not the menu. If we wish to quench our spiritual thirst, we must drink the waters of mystical insight for ourselves.

Mystical knowledge is not a collection of facts to be studied. It is a state of *knowing*. It is immediate and alive. It is natural and open to all of us, regardless of our level of education and intellectual sophistication. Jesus was the son of a carpenter, the mystical poet Kabir was a weaver and the guru Sri Nisargadatta was practically illiterate, yet like all such masters his teachings show a depth of understanding and astuteness of mind that only comes from a first hand experience of the nature of Reality.

Paradoxically, mystical knowledge is found through the recognition of our ignorance. The ancient Greek oracle of Delphi declared that the great mystic philosopher Socrates was the wisest man alive, because he knew he knew nothing! St. Aquinas, the greatest theologian of the Middle Ages, abandoned unfinished the 22 volumes of his 'Summa Theologica' announcing, 'Such things have been revealed to me that now all I have written appears in my eyes as of no greater value than straw.'

Why does thou prate of God? Everything you say of him is untrue.

MEISTER ECKHART
Christian Mystic

The end of all knowledge is love.

SAI BABA
Modern Hindu mystic

11

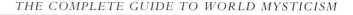

Don't you realise that if you simply have no concepts and no anxiety, you'll see the Buddha standing before you.

H U A N G - P O
Zen Master

The Islamic mystic poet Rumi described himself constructing ideas and theories like a potter making images of God from earth and water, but when he looks into the eyes of his Beloved, he wants to throw them all into the fire. When he sees God face to face, all his notions are inadequate to the beauty and vastness of his experience.

Mystical knowing is an overwhelming and blissful experience of love and rapture. The mystic looks within his heart and finds the heart of God – an all-encompassing compassion which needs no intellectual justification. As Rumi said 'When a mother cries to her suckling babe, 'Come my child, I am your mother', does the child answer, 'Oh mother, show me a proof that I will find comfort in taking your milk?'.

The reports of the mystics contained within this book are to be appreciated like poetry which inspires us through analogy and beauty and not judged as 'hard facts'. To understand the mystics we must let their words convey to us the wonder of their experience in the way that music speaks directly to the heart – we must let their insights reach deep into the soul.

The mystics of all traditions confront our most basic assumptions about ourselves and the lives we lead. They speak as individual people, yet they talk of not being confined by a physical body, or even having a separate personal identity at all. They act impeccably, yet they often question the very ideas of right and wrong, and good and bad. They seem truly free, yet they proclaim they have no will but God's will, and that this is their freedom. They do not try to convert us to a point of view, but rather to lift us beyond opinion altogether, to a more immediate intuitive understanding.

Mysticism offers a radical and individual solution to the trials and tribulations we all endure. It offers the possibility of a new life in a new world. Not by changing anything, but by simply transforming our awareness. The great mystics are the explorers of this new world, returning with extraordinary stories to challenge our common sense beliefs and stretch our imagination. There is a Hindu teaching story about a toad who lived in a well, who was one day visited by a toad who lived in the sea. 'How big is your well?' asked the first toad, 'Is it as vast as mine?'. The second toad smiled and tried to explain, 'My well is so huge that it has no edges. It contains so much water that it could never run dry in a million hot summers. It is so deep that perhaps it has no bottom.' The first toad looked incredulous, 'You are either boasting or your imagination has run away with itself!' he complained.

'Come with me,' said the sea-toad, 'and I will show you.'

1

MYSTICISM AND RELIGION

◆

Enlightenment is real,
and each one of us, whoever we are,
can in the right circumstances and with the right training
realise the nature of mind
and so know in us what is deathless and eternally pure.
This is the promise of all the mystical traditions of the world,
and it has been fulfilled and is being fulfilled
in countless thousands of human lives.
There are enlightened masters still on the earth.
When you actually meet one,
you will be shaken and moved in the depths of your heart
and you will realise that all the words
such as 'illumination' and 'wisdom',
which you thought were only ideas,
are in fact true.

SOGYAL RINPOCHE
Modern Tibetan lama

The spiral is a perennial symbol of the mystic path, found throughout nature.

MYSTICISM is not religion. It is not concerned with beliefs and doctrines, but with a natural state of consciousness which has been experienced by people of all cultures, at all times in history – by followers of every religion and of no religion. This mystical awareness is available to everyone, regardless of race, creed or culture. It is the spontaneous experience of a wider reality, beyond the limited horizon of ordinary existence. It does not invalidate the lives we are living, but rather deepens them – filling them with joy and meaning. Mystics discover a reality richer than they could have dreamed of. They are immersed in a blissful love that they know to be the very foundation of life. They are enveloped in a supreme oneness that can embrace all of life's contradictions. Their lives become a journey of spiritual awakening, to rediscover and live within the truth that they have glimpsed.

Mysticism is the contemplation of the essential mysteries of life. It confronts the questions that all children ask, but most adults prefer to push away: 'Who am I?', 'What is the purpose of life?' – questions that cannot be 'solved' by the rational adult mind, but only 'dissolved' into the child-like experience of mystical wonder. The mystics do not want us to have blind faith in particular religious creeds, but rather to set out on a personal exploration of consciousness.

The Islamic mystics called Sufis tell a delightful teaching story about a fictional character, Mullah Nasrudin, to show the folly of simply accepting what we are told by some authority, rather than trusting in our own experience. 'Mullah' is a term of respect meaning 'teacher', but Nasrudin is no ordinary teacher – he instructs us through his own foolishness. One day a neighbour calls on him and demands that he return a donkey he had borrowed some weeks before.

'I don't have your donkey,' rebuffs Nasrudin.

Unfortunately at that moment the donkey brays, and the neighbour exclaims, 'But I can hear the animal in your barn!'

Nasrudin looks deeply shocked. 'Would you take the word of a donkey over the word of a mullah?' he asks indignantly.

Religious authorities may say that God is this way or God is that way, and that this is right or that another way is wrong – but when the donkey brays, the mystics believe the donkey. They dare to trust their own personal experience, rather than an external authority. They question the prevailing beliefs of their culture or religious tradition. They are open to new possibilities; willing to be surprised, to have their world turned upside down, to let go of the safety of mass consciousness and embark on their own spiritual journey to find their own intuitive sense of meaning. This is why they have so often been heretics and non-conformists.

HERETICS AND NON-CONFORMISTS

Jesus was a Jewish heretic. Buddha was a Hindu heretic. The ancient Greek state executed the great philosopher Socrates for his heretical beliefs. Pythagoras was burnt to death along with most of his followers. Al-Hallaj, the tenth-century Islamic Sufi mystic, was crucified by the Muslim authorities. The thirteenth-century German mystic Meister Eckhart was prohibited from writing by the Catholic Church and eventually excommunicated a few days after his death. The sixteenth/seventeenth-century mystic Jacob Boehme, known as 'the inspired shoemaker', was chased out of his home town of Görlitz in Silesia by the Protestant authorities, who even desecrated his grave after his death. The Church of Rome tortured the Italian mystic philosopher Giordano Bruno over a period of eight years before he was burnt at the stake.

Ironically, it is by losing themselves in God that mystics find the rugged individualism courageously to follow their visions wherever they may lead, in a world usually hostile to their penetrating insight and spiritual values. The figure of the mystic appears eccentric and challenging to those who want to remain secure in the commonly accepted view of the world that happens to be prevalent at the time. This is why so many mystics have been forced to live precarious lives on the edges of social acceptability.

While some managed to maintain an uneasy alliance with the religious authorities of their day, most mystics were vilified and horribly persecuted for claiming direct personal knowledge of a God whom the religious establishment wished to make accessible only via their hierarchy of priests and theologians. Yet the natural experience of

The inquisition was set up to eradicate the Cathars, a medieval flowering of early Christian gnosticism.

spiritual awakening that lies at the heart of mysticism is the birthplace of all religions, and they find their common ground in this common source. Mystical experiences inspired the founders and reformers of religion as well as its greatest heretics – indeed, they have often been the same people. The history of mysticism is the history of their revelations.

GIORDANO BRUNO

Born in Naples in 1548, Giordano Bruno believed that the earth revolves around the sun, just as the soul revolves around God. He is respected as both a great mystic and an early scientist. As a young man Bruno studied to be a Dominican friar, but was expelled from his seminary for writing to a friend a note which read *'Mundus nihil pulcherium'* – 'The world is a beautiful nothing.' He was greatly influenced by the rediscovery of pagan manuscripts, particularly works attributed to the ancient Egyptian sage Thrice-Great Hermes. Bruno set off to spread this ancient mysticism throughout Europe. He inspired the creation of many secret societies including the Giordanisti, which became the Rosicrucians, the most famous of all occult fraternities; his influence can also be seen in the Egyptian imagery of seventeenth-century Scottish Freemasonry.

Bruno believed that the Egyptian religion of Hermes was the ancestor of the Greek Mystery Schools, the Jewish religion of Moses, and the birthplace of Christianity. In Bruno's imagination it was poised to become the unifying religion in which Jews, Catholic and Greek Orthodox Christians, the Platonic Humanists, and even the Muslims could meet and resolve their differences. But in his naiveté he returned to Italy and was arrested and tortured by the Roman Church. In 1600 he was ceremonially burnt alive in Rome.

A BRIEF HISTORY OF MYSTICISM

Mysticism begins with the extraordinary experiences of the ancient shamans of the primal peoples who, through the use of ritual and psychedelic plants, began an exploration of the mysteries of consciousness. In India this wisdom flowered into a profound philosophy which gradually influenced the whole of the ancient world. Ancient Egypt also developed a similar mysticism, which gave birth to the Mystery Schools – spiritual 'universities' for mystical initiation. The philosophies of India and Egypt came together in ancient Greece. Here, the Mystery Schools flourished as a religion for a thousand years, and left a legacy that would inspire all subsequent Western mystics.

The relationship of mysticism to religion has been characterized by a cycle of living revelation bringing life to dead tradition, only to fall in turn into religious orthodoxy. In sixth-century BC India, the Buddha experienced enlightenment and challenged the authorities of the Hindu religion, becoming the founder of a new mystical faith. In China, his contemporary Lao Tzu revitalized the Taoist tradition with profound mystical ideas. In the first century AD the Jewish mystic Jesus challenged the spiritual authority of the religious hierarchy in Israel, and initiated the Christian religion. Whilst the mystical spirit can still be found in all these faiths up until the present day, they have all to a greater or lesser degree slipped into the dogma and superstition of religion.

Each mystical tradition has gone through different high points and low points. Jewish mysticism reached its heights with the Kabbalists of the Middle Ages and the Hasids of the eighteenth century. Christian mysticism was most vibrant among the early Gnostics of the first century AD and the Friends of God of the thirteenth and fourteenth centuries. Islamic mysticism flowered with the Sufis of the tenth to twelfth centuries. All traditions have had their great saints and sages, who directly experienced the eternal truth and left a legacy of spiritual inspiration for those who followed. However, it is only India, the mother of mysticism, which has continually produced numbers of great enlightened masters. India's influence has once again been felt in the modern West. After the explosive increase in the use of mind-altering drugs in the 1960s, huge numbers of people looked again to the East to find a spiritual context for their strange experiences, inspiring the new wave of mysticism we are witnessing today.

In the modern world, there is growing disillusionment with orthodox dogmatic religion and scientific materialism: neither can satisfy the deep inner yearning of the soul. This has led to a profound spiritual hunger. The mystics offer us their personal testimonies that this hunger can be satisfied through a direct experience of the mystical dimensions of life. This vision may be glimpsed through the window of any one of their accounts of rapture and their inspired insights. These are the gifts of wisdom that we have inherited from those great souls who have pierced the veil of everyday reality, and beheld the timeless mystical truth.

ONE TRUTH

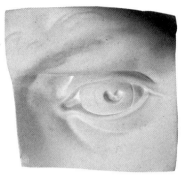

Detail of Michaelangelo's
David *with heart shaped pupil.*

Although all mystics do not have identical experiences, they all participate in the same mystery. The deeper their revelation, the more the superficially different aspects of their experiences cease to matter. To mature mystics, the bizarre and fantastic are of little interest and are sometimes no more than distractions. Beyond the amazing, they discover something simpler and more substantial – an all-embracing love, an all-consuming Oneness. Like different-coloured rays refracted through a prism, their visions are coloured by the culture and personality of the particular mystic and the depth of his or her understanding. But they find their common source in one light. This light may be called God, Buddha-Nature, Tao, Brahman, Allah or any other name, according to the culture and tradition of the mystic. But regardless of the terminology, it remains what it is. Something has been perceived, but not by the senses. Something has been understood, but not by the rational intellect. It is beyond names and concepts. This is why the Native Americans call it 'Great Mystery'.

Although the revelations that the mystics describe have a universal quality, not all the traditions are identical. Each has its particular spiritual practices, philosophical concepts and idiosyncratic vocabulary. Yet, although different paths may be followed, the destination is common to all. As Rumi writes, 'The lamps are many, but the light is One.' The modern Hindu sage Sai Baba teaches: 'All religions are facets of One Truth. All religions speak of a part of God and then assert that their part is full and total. To assume that God responds to one name only and can be adored in one form only is a sacrilege.'

ONE MYSTICAL TRADITION

The great mystic traditions of the world are similar not only because they stem from the same essential transcendental experience, but also because from time immemorial they have been in communication. For example, ancient Greece, the birthplace of Western culture, was deeply influenced by contact with ancient India, the birthplace of Eastern spirituality. Even Jesus, who is usually pictured growing up in an exclusively Jewish environment, lived less than thirty miles from cities which housed famous schools of mystical Greek philosophy and wandering saints and sages of many ancient religions. Indeed, the first language of Jesus's Galilee was Greek.

Every mystical tradition has developed within its own religious context and through important moments of historical contact and interaction with other traditions. Because many of these groups were heretical, however, much of this cross-fertilization was a secret affair; as a result their history has, until recently, remained hidden and generally unknown. It is now becoming clear that there may be many mystical paths but there is essentially only one tradition, with a common content and history: a perennial mystical philosophy, expressing itself in different words and concepts according to the culture of its origin; one timeless truth. The fifteenth-century mystic Cardinal Nicholas of Cusa wrote: 'Never has there existed a people so ignorant which believed in a plurality of gods and did not also admit some One Divinity, Supreme Principle, or Creator of the Universe. Humanity will find that it is not a diversity of creeds, but the same creed which is everywhere presupposed.'

For the mystic who has seen the wider vision, religious divisions are tragically ridiculous. The fanatics and fundamentalists who pit one creed against another are like the four blind men in an old Indian teaching story, who, stumbling upon an elephant for the first time, set about exploring their discovery.

One man takes hold of the elephant's trunk. 'This animal is a type of snake', he reports.

'You are wrong,' says the next, while touching the elephant's ear, 'it is like a great leaf.'

'Nonsense,' counters the third as he lays his hands on the elephant's leg. 'This animal is like a tree trunk'.

'How confused you all are,' the last blind man exclaims whilst passing the elephant's tail between his palms. 'It is as thin as a piece of rope.'

The four men start to argue bitterly until a sighted man happens to pass by. Observing their disagreements in amazement, he explains, 'An elephant is all of these things and more – can't you see?'

Like the bee gathering honey from different flowers, the wise man accepts the essence of different scriptures and sees only the good in all religions.

The Srimad Bhagavatam
(The Wisdom of God)

2

SHAMANIC MYSTICISM

---◆---

Nothing I have ever seen with my eyes
was so clear and bright as what my vision showed me;
and no words that I ever heard with my ears
are like the words I heard.
I did not have to remember these things;
they remembered themselves all these years.
It was as I grew older
that the meaning came clearer and clearer
out of the pictures and the words;
and even now I know that more was shown to me
than I can tell.

BLACK ELK
Nineteenth-century Native American mystic

S HAMANISM is the most ancient form of mysticism and the root of all later spiritual traditions. It is still found in the cultures of the primal peoples all over the world. The word 'shaman' is a name of Mongol origin used by the Siberian tribes to signify someone who has access to other spiritual dimensions. It has now come to be used as a general name for all such mystics amongst primal peoples. Shamans have the power to heal and sometimes to harm, to make prophecies, to receive visions and to penetrate the mysteries of life and death. They claim to be able to fly, and to communicate with animals, nature spirits and the power of life. Shamans induce ecstatic trances by sacred rituals, drumming, song, communing with nature, consuming hallucinogenic plants and other magical techniques. In these mystical states, the shaman transcends his personal identity and becomes a representative of his tribal group in the spiritual world.

The Serpent of Immortality *is an ancient symbol of healing and is still in use today. Two serpents entwined is the symbol of the British Medical Association.*

There is evidence of shamanic practices amongst the very earliest human beings. Skeletons found in Neolithic (Stone Age) graves, for example, are often curled up like a foetus and buried with flowers, suggesting that death was seen as a form of rebirth. This symbolism is still found today amongst the Babawa people of Zaire in central Africa. As a man is dying a woman sits back to back with him on her heels with her legs wide open, as if giving birth to him in the spirit world. The realization that a human being is more than a mortal body gives meaning to this transitory life and transforms it into a spiritual journey of discovering that which does not die. Most shamanic cultures see this journey as being made through many lives, with each soul reincarnating over and over again. The belief in reincarnation has been retained and developed by nearly all the later mystical traditions of the world, including those of Hindus, Buddhists, ancient Mystery School pagans, early Christian Gnostics and later Christian Cathars, Jewish Kabbalists and Islamic Sufis.

ABORIGINAL SHAMANISM

The closest we can come to understanding the mysticism of our ancient ancestors is to look at the practices of the Aboriginal peoples of Australia, whose traditional way of life has not changed substantially for over thirty-five thousand years. The human consciousness after death is described by Aboriginal Shamans as 'survival in infinity'. To prepare for death by experiencing this awareness while they are alive, elders will often leave the community to retreat alone into the mountains where they practise various mystical techniques such as 'Sky Gazing'. This is a natural form of meditation which involves staring into the sky to achieve a spacious awareness within which, they say, consciousness is no longer in the body but reflected in the whole cosmos. Aborigines call such mystical states 'The Dreaming'.

The shaman, whom the Aborigines call a Karadji or 'Clever Man', is someone who is particularly adept at entering altered states of consciousness. He usually receives a call to be a shaman in a dream, but in order to develop his spiritual awareness he must undergo a harrowing initiation in which he will ritually die to his mortal self and be reborn in spirit. According to the Arunta and Aranda peoples, an initiate goes to the mouth of a special cave where the spirits visit him. They pierce him with invisible spears through the tongue, through the neck, and from ear to ear. The spirits carry him, now 'dead', into the cave, where they remove all his vital organs and replace them with new ones, along with special quartz crystals on which his magic will later depend. He is now 'reborn' as a Karadji.

By going into trance states he may now communicate with spirit-beings, cure sickness and 'fly' into the spirit world. Clever Men are said to have an invisible cord of flame which connects them to Baime, the All-Father Sky God. The mysterious wind-like whining sound made by a whirling bullroarer is said to be the voice of Baime, and a Karadji whirls a bullroarer over a fire at the centre of a sacred circle to induce visions of God in the flames. In addition to bullroarers these shamans use drums, click sticks and didgeridoos, accompanied by rhythmic dancing, symbolic actions and the smoking of sacred herbs, to induce mystic trances. In ecstatic states these shamans are immune to pain, and can roll in hot coals without being burnt.

FACING FEAR

In the cultures of all primal peoples, shamanic initiation is a terrifying affair. Amongst the Yurak-Samoyed of Siberia the future shaman is initiated by lying unconscious for seven day and nights while he is dismembered by spirits. Characteristically, a shaman receives a spontaneous calling while still young. Often this experience itself is terrifying. A Nepalese shaman called Bhirendra, talking in 1914, recalled his dramatic initiatory calling at the age of thirteen. He

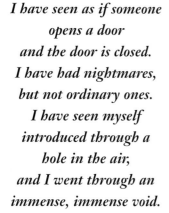

I have seen as if someone opens a door and the door is closed. I have had nightmares, but not ordinary ones. I have seen myself introduced through a hole in the air, and I went through an immense, immense void.

E D U A R D O
Modern Peruvian shaman

described becoming possessed by a spirit who he later discovered was his dead grandfather. Mad with possession, he began to shake uncontrollably and ran off naked into the woods. He recounted his bizarre experience in these words:

The horned priest, the sacred bull and the spirit of the elements are Shamanic symbols that embody elemental powers.

> *My grandfather and the other spirits all wore pointed hats and were only three feet tall. They taught me magical mantras and passed on to me sacred energies. They fed me earthworms and I had to eat them or die. Still, each time I tried to reach for the worms one of the spirit wives (who are monstrous-looking) whipped my hands. She carried a gold sword and every time she whipped me she yelled, 'Let's cut off his head.' My grandfather said no because he wanted to teach me.*

Having survived this first encounter, the young Bhirendra ran off again, this time to a cemetery. He armed himself with a magic dagger which belonged to his father, who was a shaman. In the cemetery Bhirendra saw many evil spirits, some with long crooked fangs, others with no heads and with eyes in the middle of their chests, and still others carrying decaying corpses. He related:

> *They attacked me and before I knew it, they were all over me devouring my body. I was scared to death and, in a last hope, cried for the gods to save me, pleading that I was only a young boy. I drew my father's magical dagger, but it fell to the ground and struck a rock. This created a spark of light and everything changed. Suddenly it was daylight and the demons were gone. I was alive!*

The Dogon Tribe of Mali became world famous in the 1970s for their astronomical knowledge of celestial objects unknown to modern science until this century. Like all primal peoples the goal of their dancing is possession by the gods.

The Tibetan Buddhists, whose religion is based on indigenous Tibetan shamanism, say that such demons are a manifestation of the initiate's own fears that he must confront and overcome in this dramatic way. He must face the ultimate fear of death and dismemberment, and in finding the courage to do so he disidentifies with his limited personal self and experiences a deeper identity, thus gaining access to spiritual states of awareness.

THE VISION QUEST

Native Americans sought mystical experiences by going on what is called a Vision Quest. No one, it was believed, could have success in their life without a personal vision. After an extended period of preparation, including the ritual use of a sweat lodge, fasting and other forms of purification, the quester was left alone on a mountainside for four days and nights. Traditionally he had neither food nor water, and only a blanket to keep out the cold. Here he faced fear, loneliness and doubt. This was a time of trial, after which he would never be the same again.

He was spiritually watched over by an experienced shaman, who performed ritual mystical practices at this time. The quester always remained within a prescribed magical circle, which he was not allowed to leave on any account. He focused continually on his desire for a vision, and ideally did not sleep but prayed and sang sacred songs. In some traditions he may have performed hard manual labour, such as lifting heavy stones, to weaken his body and open his spirit to the visionary world. He may even have cut his flesh or amputated a finger.

In a mystical practice called the Night of Fear, the quester dug his own grave in some remote spot and lay in it all night. The sounds of the night and the darkness stimulated all his fears – especially that of death. This he sought to confront and overcome, so that he could be spiritually reborn into an intuitive knowledge of his immortal soul. Through such shamanic practices the Native Americans directly sought mystical experiences in which they transcended their limited self and discovered the Oneness of Great Spirit – Wakan Tanka. Black Elk says: 'Peace comes within the Souls of men when they realize their relationship, their Oneness, with the Universe and all its powers; and when they realize that at the center of the Universe dwells Wakan Tanka, and that this center is really everywhere. It is within each of us.'

Let us see is this Real,
Let us see is this Real,
This Life I am living.

Native American chant

THE SWEAT LODGE

The Native American sweat lodge, used for physical and spiritual purification, was a small, dark enclosure in which hot stones were covered in water to create a steam bath. On the Great Plains sweat lodges were temporary structures of willow poles covered in buffalo hides, while in the North-West they were often made of cedar planks covered in birch bark. In California they were both a ceremonial centre and a dwelling place.

The sweat lodge is in effect a sacred womb from which the participants emerge spiritually reborn, and it is not unique to North America. The Celts made them of sods and stones. In northern Russia they were constructed of wood, sometimes partially or totally underground. The ancient Japanese had ceremonial steam baths called *mushi-buro*, and steam purification is widely practised in Africa. Homer talks of *laconia*, which became the *balneum* of the Romans and in the Arab world the famous Turkish baths. Such places were originally revered as sacred, and there is an old Finnish saying that goes: 'In the sauna one must conduct oneself as if one were in church.'

THE SUN DANCE

Amongst Native Americans, the whole tribe shared in mystical practices such as the sun dance. It was a dance of courage and sacrifice, in which every element carried a profound symbolic meaning. The men first purified themselves in a sweat lodge and by fasting for three days. Before the dance began, each participant's pectoral muscles were ceremonially pierced with a cherrywood spike, which was connected by a thong to the sun dance tree located in the centre of the dancing circle. He would then dance without stopping for four days and four nights. To fall was a great disgrace, and a bad omen for the whole tribe. He would on no account stop, even when, through his wild movements, the cherrywood spike eventually ripped through the skin of his chest.

By willingly suffering in this way, the dancers conquered suffering. While the men danced, the women cut small pieces of their flesh from their forearms to honour the dancers and share in the ceremony. The men blew whistles made of eagle bones, which made a sound like an eagle's cry. The eagle is a sacred bird which, because it flies so high and sees so clearly, symbolically embodies Great Spirit. The drums, the fasting, the dancing and the sacredness of the occasion all induced mystical visions in the participants. As the dawn broke, the dancers greeted the new rays by ecstatically singing:

> *Here am I – behold me.*
> *I am the sun – behold me.*

The Native Americans used such rituals to awaken an awareness of Wakan Tanka. Religion was not a 'tradition' but a living experience of a living divine presence. The Dwamish chief Seattle, speaking in 1854, said, 'Our religion is the dreams of our old men, given to them in the solemn hours of the night by the Great Spirit; and the visions of our Medicine Men; and it is written in the hearts of the people.'

SACRED TOBACCO

Shamans of all cultures use plants and herbs for healing and magical purification, as well as for their intoxicating qualities. Tobacco is the most sacred herb of the Native Americans and is used in most of their spiritual ceremonies. The pipe is a sacred artefact, and the whole process of smoking is charged with mystical symbolic significance. Smoking makes the breath visible, and breath is the very source of life.

Black Elk's lifetime saw the utter destruction of the Native American culture. His vision, however, is still alive and inspires a growing number of modern Americans.

BLACK ELK

The Native American Sioux visionary Black Elk had an extraordinary life. As a young man he fought with Sitting Bull and Crazy Horse in the great Sioux victory over General Custer. Later he watched the gradual defeat and decline of his people and their culture. As a performer in Buffalo Bill's Wild West Circus he travelled to England and met 'Mother England' – Queen Victoria. Returning to America, he witnessed the brutal massacre at Wounded Knee.

During a childhood illness he experienced a profound vision: 'While I stood there I saw more than I can tell and understood more than I saw; for I was seeing in a sacred manner the shapes of all things in spirit, and the shape of all shapes as they must live together like one being.' Speaking of a visionary encounter with a Spirit of the Earth, Black Elk reports that he stared at the spirit, feeling that he knew him. As he did so the vision slowly changed as if the spirit were growing backwards into its youth. When it had finally become a boy, Black Elk recognized it as himself.

Those who share a pipe acknowledge that they share the same air – the same life. The inhalation and exhalation of smoke is the ebb and flow of existence. Smoke is taken into the body and then released, carrying prayers up to Great Spirit as it rises into the air.

To be a pipe carrier is a responsibility and an honour, comparable to being a priest, and is earned through initiation and spiritual instruction. The pipe is more than simply functional – its form encodes the mystical wisdom of the tribe. The bowl represents the female aspect of Great Spirit, while the phallic stem symbolizes the male aspect. Bringing these two together represents the ultimate oneness of God. The tobacco which is burnt to ash symbolizes all that changes, and the stem represents all that is absolute and permanent. When a Native American smokes a pipe, he is aware of all this symbolism; he is partaking in a sacred mystery.

The modern Sioux medicine man Lame Deer says:

For us Indians there is just the pipe, the earth we sit on, and the open sky. The spirit is everywhere. That smoke from the peace pipe, it goes straight up to the spirit world. But this is a two-way thing. Power flows down to us through that smoke, through the pipe stem. You feel that power as you hold the pipe; it moves from the pipe right into your body. It makes your hair stand up. That pipe is not just a thing; it is alive.

The white man goes into his church house and talks about Jesus. The Indian goes into his teepee, and talks to Jesus.

Native American saying

PSYCHEDELIC PLANTS

The use of hallucinogenic or psychedelic plants to induce profound mystical revelations is commonplace amongst the shamanic cultures of the primal peoples. To them, there could be nothing more natural or straightforward than eating a particular mushroom or cactus, or smoking a certain herb and through this plant experiencing mystical rapture and ecstatic visions. 'Psychedelic' means 'mind-expanding', or, more accurately, 'soul-enlarging'. From the Indians of the Amazon to the shamans of Siberia, all these cultures pay homage to the psychedelic bounty of the natural world. In these cultures, 'drugs' are seen as an organic manifestation of the mystical power of God. The anthropologist Michael Harner writes, 'Undoubtedly one of the major reasons that anthropologists for so long underestimated the importance of hallucinogenic substances in Shamanism and religious experience was that very few had partaken themselves of the native psychotropic materials.'

The mushroom *Amanita muscaria*, commonly known as fly agaric, is used by Siberian shamans. It is the archetypal fairy toadstool of children's stories, with a big red cap covered in white spots. The image of pixies living under such mushrooms is a remnant of the use of fly agaric by European Shamans many hundreds of years ago to induce visions of elemental nature sprites – the 'fairy folk' experienced by Celtic mystics in psychedelic revelations. The rich spirituality recorded in the ancient Hindu scriptures called the *Vedas* finds its roots in the shamanic use of soma, a milky drink prepared from fly agaric. The writer of the *Rig Veda*, one of the four books which comprise the *Vedas*, enthuses, 'I have drunk Soma, I have become immortal', proclaiming:

> *I have passed beyond sky and earth in my glory,*
> *Have I been drinking Soma?*
> *I will lift up the earth and put it here or there,*
> *Have I been drinking Soma?*

The poet and mythologist Robert Graves became convinced, after scholarly investigation and his own personal experiences, that fly agaric was the basis of the 'nectar' and 'ambrosia' used as mystical intoxicants by the ancient Greek Mystery Schools. The Greek civilization was a development from the Mycenaean culture – Mycenae means 'Mushroom City'. When intoxicated by psychedelic mushrooms, the devotees of the nature god Dionysus were called 'maenads' or 'maddened ones'. They celebrated the autumn, when the first mushrooms appeared, with a festival.

The priestess of the Oracle at Delphi in ancient Greece used hashish to enter into a trance from which she delivered the prophecies of the god Apollo. Such oracles were consulted by great kings and statesmen on political matters, but were also centres of mystic initiation and schools of philosophy. The great Greek philosopher Plato wrote, 'Consider all the benefits which individuals and states in Greece have received from the Priestesses when they were intoxicated, although their usefulness in their sober senses amounts to little or nothing.' The evidence overwhelmingly suggests that, like all cultures still in touch with their shamanic roots, the Greeks regarded psychedelic plants as great gifts of God, capable of inducing real spiritual insight.

SHAMANISM TODAY

The Amanita Muscaria *mushroom haunts the popular imagination in thousands of children's picture books. It is still used today by Asian shaman as a 'powerful ally'.*

Psychedelic plants are still used in shamanic traditions today. The Native American Church, a modern synthesis of South American psychedelic shamanism, European Christianity and Native American spiritual traditions, uses peyote, a hallucinogenic cactus, to induce mystical visions. The road man is the priest of the peyote meeting; he represents Great Spirit and reveals the Peyote Road to the worshippers. A Native American user of peyote says of his experience: 'The whole world is in there. When I am looking at this fine little peyote here, my mind is praying. I can't think of nothing bad. All is good. It is the music the Creator put on earth to make the minds of humans good and clear.'

To put herself in contact with the other world, the modern Mexican shaman-priestess Maria Sabrina practises night-long chanting and clapping ceremonies under the influence of the psychedelic mushroom teonanacatl. She describes the ecstatic visions which it induces in these terms: 'The more you go inside the world of Teonanacatl, the more things are seen. And you also see our past and future, which are there already as a single thing already achieved, already happened. . . . Millions of things I saw and knew. I knew and saw God.' To know God is the highest goal of all shamanic practices and of all mysticism.

Shamanism is the oldest form of all spiritual traditions. It has no scriptures, ecclesiastical hierarchies or dogmas, but rather points to the power of life all around us in the organic processes of birth and death. By simply gazing at the sky, playing primitive instruments and ingesting psychedelic plants our ancestors began an exploration of consciousness which has been continued by all the great saints and sages that have followed in their footsteps. Today, shamanic mystical practices such as drumming, chanting, sweat lodge purification and vision questing are again becoming popular in the modern West as it searches for its ancient spiritual roots.

3

HINDU MYSTICISM

Fear not, wise one! You are not in danger.
There is a way to cross the ocean of life and death,
through which the saints have gained the other shore.
This way I will reveal to you.

The stupid man looks at his body and says, 'This is I.'
The more learned thinks, 'This is I' of his personality.
But the wise man knows the true Self, saying, 'I am the Eternal.'
He is individual, though without separateness.
He who possesses Soul vision
has dissolved the 'I' in Pure Consciousness.

To those who are wandering in this desert world,
weary, oppressed and worn by sorrow,
may this teaching reveal the Eternal Oneness,
bringing joy, like an ocean of nectar near at hand.

SANKARA
Eighth-century Hindu saint

All Hindus revere the sacred symbol OM *and millions chant this powerful mantra every day.*

WHILST INDIA is materially amongst the poorest countries in the world today, spiritually it is fabulously wealthy. Its riches are its saints and sages, who since ancient times have been practical living proof of the reality of mystical enlightenment. Hinduism, the principal religion of India, is as full of charlatans as any other. Yet despite this, it has remained a vibrant and unrivalled source of genuine mystical spirituality. India is alive with holy men and miracle workers. Stories of people having strange psychic powers, bilocating (being seen in two places at once), healing and even raising the dead are not just mythical tales from ancient history, but are claimed to have happened in recent years and have been witnessed by large numbers of respected citizens. India's scriptures are the oldest in the world, yet in the twentieth century it has produced as many great spiritual beings as at any other time in the country's history.

In Western culture, whilst the outer forms of religion are still given lip service, the idea that the mystical journey could be the very purpose of life is seen as eccentric and even abnormal. In India it is a commonplace. Countless wandering renunciates called Sannyasins, who have abandoned the world to search for God, possessing nothing and clothed in simple orange robes, pass from village to village. In India they are not regarded as beggars or parasites, but respected and admired. They are willingly fed and looked after, for there is still a general belief that to serve a spiritual seeker is a holy act which will also benefit the donor. Spiritual centres called ashrams, usually presided over by a guru or spiritual teacher, thrive throughout India.

Although some Indians take it more seriously than others, travelling the mystic path is a normal part of everyday life. Millions bathe in the holy River Ganges to purify themselves. Huge numbers of ordinary people have a guru and regularly perform some sort of spiritual practice. It is not unusual on retirement for Hindus to enter a completely new phase of life – withdrawing from the world to concentrate on God, giving up their name and relinquishing their social and family roles, so that they may spiritually prepare themselves for death.

Spirituality informs all aspects of Indian life. Indeed, the inspiration and founding father of the modern state of India, through the power which he called Satyagraha, or the Truth-Force, was a great mystic. Mohandas Gandhi lived a life of complete renunciation. He owned

If men thought of God as much as they think of the world who would not obtain liberation?

Maitri Upanishad

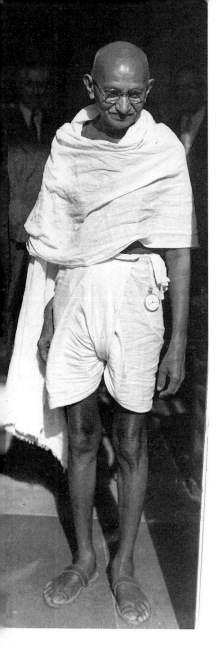

nothing: when he died he had only two dollars to his name and weighed 100 pounds. Through compassion to all forms of life he was a strict fruitarian. He knew every word of the Hindu scripture the *Bhagavad Gita* by heart. He espoused non-violence and loved his enemies. He led his people through selfless service, and preached the unity of all religions. Much to his embarrassment, he became known as 'Mahatma' – *Maha Atman*, meaning 'Great Soul'. When he was assassinated by a Hindu fundamentalist, he died with the name of God on his lips. Gandhi was a living embodiment of the mystic path. Once asked by a journalist to give a message to the world, he scribbled on a piece of paper, 'My life is my message.' It is hard to imagine such a figure in any other country but India.

ONE GOD, MANY FACES

Hinduism is polytheistic – it has many gods and goddesses. This is very often misunderstood as primitive superstition, inferior to monotheistic religions such as Judaism, Christianity and Islam that believe in one God. All polytheistic cultures, however, also believe in one supreme God; Hindus usually call this entity Brahman. This ultimate divinity, which is indescribable, impersonal and abstract, is seen as manifesting in a plethora of gods and goddesses who embody different divine qualities. These deities are like different faces worn by the faceless impersonal divine power, so that human beings can relate to him/her/it in a more personal way, enabling them to follow an aspect of God which suits their own needs and temperament.

An Indian tour guide was once asked by a foreign tourist, 'Why do you Hindus have ridiculous statues of gods and goddesses with so many faces?'

The guide replied, 'We Hindus believe that every person is a face of God. My regret is that we are able to show so few faces on our statues.'

Because of this polytheism, Hinduism is an extremely tolerant and all-embracing faith. It acknowledges other religions as other ways to the same supreme God. Different faiths and their prophets can be welcomed and accepted, because all seeming contradictions in their teachings are seen as largely irrelevant. It is simply like one person saying, 'To climb the mountain from this place you must turn right, then left', and another person starting from a different spot announcing, 'To make the ascent from here you must turn left, then right.' The summit remains the same, and any path that leads there is of

Mahatma Ghandi died owning two dollars and weighing 100 pounds. With the simple power of his presence he changed the course of history.

OPPOSITE: *A pilgrim at Mount Kailash in Tibet. From Mount Olympus to Mount Fuji in Japan, sacred mountains are revered as the home of the gods by all cultures.*

VARDHAMANA AND THE JAINS

There are today about three million Jains, almost all of whom live in India. They have become extremely influential, not least through Mahatma Gandhi who, although not himself a Jain, grew up in a Jain community and adopted their doctrine of *ahimsa* – non-violence. For the Jains, to injure any living being is to attract harmful Karma. They are therefore strict vegetarians and often wear masks and sweep the street before them as they walk, to prevent them unintentionally killing small insects. As Buddhists follow the Buddha, so Jains follow the Jina, which means 'The Conqueror' – a title given to Vardhamana, the last of the great Jain teachers. It is also used to signify any man or woman who has transcended himself or herself and become spiritually perfected.

Vardhamana, who was also known as Mahavira, 'The Great Hero', was undoubtedly an actual historical person. He was born about 540 BC and died around 468 BC. He was slightly older than the Buddha, and many of the stories told of his life are remarkably similar to those told of the Buddha. Both of them, for example, are said to have been educated as a prince and married a princess, only to reject the world to adopt an ascetic life. For thirteen years Vardhamana wore just a simple loincloth, eventually discarding this as well to go about naked for the rest of his life. When he was about forty he underwent a long fast and attained enlightenment.

value. The twentieth-century Hindu mystic Sri Aurobindo writes: 'That which we call the Hindu religion is really the eternal religion because it embraces all others.'

The great nineteenth-century mystic Ramakrishna, who saw God in everyone and everything, said:

I have practised all religions – Hinduism, Islam, Christianity – and I have also followed the paths of various sects of Hinduism. I have found that it is the same God toward whom all are turned, all along different roads. Everywhere I see men who dispute in the name of religion. But they do not stop to think that he who is called Krishna is also called Shiva, and that he is also called Primal Force or Jesus or Allah. The substance is One under different names, and each man is looking for the same substance.

OPPOSITE: *In this Buddhist Mandala we see the many wrathful demons and compassionate gods that inhabit the Buddhist heavens. The Mandala is a powerful symbol of the unity that embraces all diversity and is used in Tibet as an aid to meditation.*

THE ETERNAL TEACHINGS

Hinduism has no founder, no one spiritual leader, no organized hierarchy of priests and no body of orthodox doctrines. Instead, at its heart is the idea of personal salvation through a direct experience of God. There is plenty of room for the kind of mystical individualism which many other religions seek to suppress. 'Hindu' is the Persian word for 'Indian'. The Indians themselves prefer to speak of their faith as Sanatana Dharma – the Eternal Teaching of the Law. As a popular religion Hinduism is like any other, with its quirks and peculiarities, its rituals and rites, its concepts and vocabulary. Its perennial mystical philosophy, however, has since ancient times been an inspiration to the world.

It gave birth to Buddhism, which spread north to Tibet and east to China and Japan. Successive generations of ancient Greek sages travelled to India and returned with mystical teachings that formed the basis of the Greek Mystery religion (see Chapter 6). Zeus and Tiu, respectively the chief Greek and Teutonic gods, and the Latin name for a god, *deus*, are all derived from the Sanskrit Indian name Dyaus, meaning 'The Shining One' or simply 'The Light'. From the ancient Mystery Schools, Indian philosophy deeply influenced Christian and

THE PARSEES

The name 'Parsee' means 'Persians', and refers to believers in the 3500-year-old Zoroastrian religion. In the face of Muslim persecution in the ninth century the Parsees left Persia for India, a journey which they believe was part of the divine plan. The Parsees honour fire as the symbol of Ahura Mazda, the One-God preached by the prophet Zoroaster. The prayer room in a fire temple is bare of all decoration so that attention is fixed on the living image of God – 'the pure flame of the fire symbolizing him who is himself eternal light'.

In the early twentieth century a Parsee called Behraqmshah Shroff (1857–1927) reinvigorated the mystical roots of his religion. He claimed to have been taken by a wandering group of secret Zoroastrians to caves in the Persian mountains where he was shown ancient treasures and teachings. Upon his return he was silent for thirty years, but subsequently taught his followers 'Ilm-i Kshnoom' – the 'Path of Knowledge'. Today there are some two hundred thousand Parsees.

Islamic mystical spirituality. In our own century there has been a new wave of Indian mysticism sweeping the West, with many gurus visiting or taking up residence in Europe and America, initiating hundreds of thousands into the mystical path.

Hinduism developed from primal shamanic practices such as the spiritual use of sacred psychedelic plants. Of the four books of the ancient Hindu scriptures called the *Vedas*, the *Rig Veda* is the largest. The thousand hymns which it comprises contain over nine hundred references to soma, the hallucinogenic preparation mentioned in Chapter 2. By directly communing with nature through the use of such plants, the ancients opened doorways into other states of awareness. They saw through the veil of physical reality and began an exploration of inner space. The fruit of these early mystical experiences was further distilled into the wisdom of the *Upanishads* – a collection of scriptures written in the eighth century BC. They are

The Hindu god Shiva, often pictured with a necklace of skulls, embodies the destroying aspects of the cosmos. The circle of life in which the god dances cannot be complete without death, from which comes new life.

35

sometimes called the 'Himalayas of the Soul' in honour of their towering mystical magnitude.

By the time of the *Upanishads*, the many Hindu gods and goddesses were seen as presided over by God in three aspects – Brahma the Creator, Vishnu the Preserver and Shiva the Destroyer. Vishnu is believed to take on a human body from time to time, so that he may reawaken in mankind a love of the truth. These divine incarnations are called avatars. Most famous is his incarnation as Krishna, the powerful teacher of the *Bhagavad Gita*, an important Hindu mystical scripture written in the sixth century.

Vishnu is believed to have taken many human forms, not only in the dim mythological past but right up to the present day. There have been many masters this century who have been revered as divine avatars, such as Sai Baba and Krishnamurti, who later rejected this title. To a Westerner, this can sound strange and challenging. We are used to the claim that Jesus was an incarnation of God, but the idea that this might be commonplace is quite foreign. To the Hindus, however, who believe that we are all knowing or unknowing sparks of the

KRISHNA

An endearingly beautiful, flute-playing incarnation of God, Krishna is often portrayed surrounded by milkmaids; each believes herself to be Krishna's only lover, and that she dances with him alone – a delightful image of the relationship between the soul and God. 'Hare Krishna, Hare Krishna, Hare Hare, Krishna Krishna' is a Hindu mantra sung by orange-clad devotees in most major Western cities. They are members of the Krishna Consciousness Movement, founded in 1965 by Swami Prabhupada and inspired by a sixteenth-century Bengali saint called Caitanya, who surrendered himself to Krishna and experienced raptures of intense delight.

The fifteenth-century Indian mystic poetess Mirabai wrote beautiful love poetry to Krishna, whom she called the Dark One. Written in the common language rather than Sanskrit, they are still greatly loved in India. She once travelled to visit a famous philosopher in Brindavan, the site of the most important temples to Krishna, but because she was a woman she was refused an audience. Mirabai sent a message stating that in relation to Krishna all true devotees, whether male or female, were like women in their love and adoration. The philosopher, acknowledging her wisdom and depth of devotion, consented to see her. Mirabai's teachings are that a living love of God is a more genuine spirituality than anything in the scriptures.

divine, it is not so outlandish. An avatar is a being who, unlike most of us, comes to this world not to learn but to teach the eternal mystical wisdom.

HINDU MYSTICAL WISDOM

Hinduism teaches the sublime mystical truth, that at the heart of every man and woman is a divine soul. The Hindus call this *atman*. The path of mysticism is to discover the immortal *atman* that lies hidden in the mortal body. The seeker who discovers his soul will then know from direct experience the supreme mystical revelation that '*atman* is Brahman' – the self is God. This essential truth is hidden by *maya* – the illusion of separateness that obscures the underlying oneness of reality. *Maya* creates the world of appearances that we inhabit, which the mystics say is no more than a waking dream.

We are trapped in *maya* by our karma – the universal laws of cause and effect. The goal of the spiritual journey is to achieve *moksha* – liberation from karma. Karma is often interpreted as a form of cosmic justice – for each good action a person performs he will reap good fortune, and for each bad action misfortune. Hindus believe that we reincarnate into a human body over and over again, so that in this life we are experiencing the karma we have accrued in previous lives. We will continue to reincarnate, they say, until we have exhausted our karma and so become free of the cycle of birth and death.

The mystics, however, have a more profound understanding of karma. For them, to be free from karma is not to have paid off some cosmic debt. They know that there is only God who does everything – no individual self causes things to happen. The idea of personal karma accrued by personal good and bad actions is part of the illusion of being a separate self. Freedom from personal karma is simply to see that it never existed. Karma is just the natural law that the past creates the future, an impersonal process of life with which we become entangled when we believe ourselves to be separate individuals. The enlightened mystic knows himself to be pure consciousness witnessing all the events of life unfolding by God's will – including what he has taken to be 'his' thoughts and actions. Life continues through the laws of cause and effect, but not because of him and not to him. He has his being beyond such things. Such an enlightened master has no personal karma, because he knows he is not a person. He has awoken from the dream of *maya*. As it says in the *Bhagavad Gita*: 'For he who understands in Truth that he does nothing, even though he kills, it is not "he" who kills. He is not bound by Karma.'

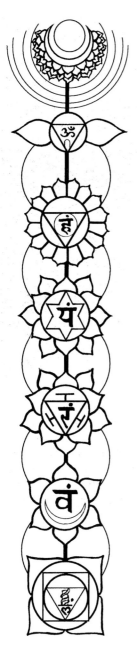

YOGA

'Yoga' means union, and the different yogas of Hinduism are all paths to escape the illusion of *maya* and attain union with the oneness of God. Hindu mystics practise a plethora of spiritual yogas to awaken mystical experiences. The most famous and widespread in the West is hatha yoga. The body is regarded as a temple of the soul, and hatha yoga teaches the use of postures and breath control to enhance all aspects of physical health and so purify and strengthen this temple. In the West this has become an end in itself. For the yogi, however, it is merely the first step on a path that leads to God.

Hatha yoga and more esoteric yogas such as kundalini also invigorate the energy body which surrounds the physical body, and in so doing produce mystical states of awareness. This energy body contains seven power points called chakras, which are associated with different states of consciousness. The word 'chakra' comes from the ancient language of Sanskrit and means 'wheel'. The chakras are centres of spinning energy, and energizing and balancing them is the central work of these yogas. They are like a natural mystic ladder which the yogi may climb to reach the highest spiritual awareness.

The two central types of yoga are that of the bhakti and the gnani – the path of love and the path of knowledge. These two ways lead to the same mystical truth, and most mystics practise elements of both. To follow the path of bhakti yoga is to lose the separate self in devotion to God. These ecstatic mystics reach enlightenment by celebrating a cosmic love affair with God. One such great bhakti was the sixteenth-century Bengali saint known as Caitanya. In mystical ecstasy he would cry, sing, shout, dance, climb trees, run about and jump up and down; he finally drowned in a holy river whilst in a fit of ecstasy. In the tradition he inspired, mystics dance and sing hymns and chant the names of God with mounting excitement, sometimes in procession through the streets, until they lose themselves in divine love.

Another influential bhakti was the fifteenth-century saint Kabir, known as 'The Despised Weaver of Benares'. Kabir was born a Muslim, yet he was the disciple of a Hindu guru. Like many great mystics, he preached that God cannot be found through the outward trappings of any religion, but only through the inward path of a sincere and open heart. He taught the essential unity of all genuine spirituality and is therefore honoured by both Hindu and Islamic mystics. His devotional songs and poems are still popular in India, opening the heart of the listener to a sublime love for God. He writes ecstatically:

Activating 'power points' within the body (called Chakras in sanscrit) is the aim of Yoga. The seven chakras ascend from the base of the spine to the top of the head and are depicted as spinning wheels of energy.

What can the eunuch know
Of the happiness of the bride and bridegroom?
What can the ignorant know
Of the bliss of God-realisation?
What can they know, these worldly fools,
These fools, fools, fools?

I will take you into my confidence:
Love can be purchased across the counter,
But the price is your head. Still, that's very cheap.
Don't waste a moment in buying it.

The path of gnani yoga is to see through the illusion of separateness and know the underlying oneness of God. This is done through stilling the mind in meditation, by constantly asking profound questions such as 'Who am I?', and by immersing the intellect in mystical philosophy. This path was definitively expressed by the eighth-century mystic Sankara, a wandering sage who became the most influential of all Hindu philosophers. Like many great mystics, Sankara was a child prodigy. At the age of five he became a Brahmin priest, and knew all the *Vedas* by heart. When he was eight he was initiated into an ascetic order. In his short life of thirty-two years he became revered as a great saint. In one of his most famous works, called *Atma Bodhi* which means 'Know Your Self', he vividly describes the experience of mystical union with God:

An Indian Yogi practises Hatha Yoga in India. Yoga teaches control and purification of the body as the first step along the mystical path. Yoga has now become very popular in the West.

My mind fell like a hailstone into the vast expanse of Brahman's ocean. Touching one drop of it, I melted away and became one with Brahman. This is wonderful indeed! Here is the ocean of Brahman, full of endless joy. How can I accept or reject anything? Is there anything apart or distinct from Brahman? Now, finally and clearly, I know that I am the atman, *whose nature is eternal joy. I see nothing. I hear nothing. I know nothing that is separate from me.*

MANTRA

A mantra is a word or phrase with spiritual power. Bhaktis chant mantras as part of their devotional practices, and gnanis often use them as an object of meditation. By repeating a mantra over and over again the mystic stills his restless and distracted thoughts, concentrating his attention on God. This is a powerful doorway into the mystic experience. Any word or phrase that has spiritual resonance for the

As well as OM, other Sanskrit mantras are used as a focus for meditation.

individual seeker can be used as a mantra. Sometimes he will be given a particular mantra by his guru to meet his particular needs. A common mantra is to repeat a name for God, such as 'Om'.

Om (pronounced A-U-M) is the most ancient word for God that has come down through the ages, and is used as a mantra by millions of people. The *Katha Upanishad* says, 'I will tell you the word that all the Vedas glorify, all self-sacrifice expresses, all sacred studies and holy life seek. That word is Om.' The *Rig Veda* states, 'In the beginning was God, with whom was the Word; and the Word was truly the supreme God.' The importance of 'Om', the primal word, can be traced through the teachings of Plato, the Greek Stoic philosophers and Philo the Jew to St John, the author of the fourth Gospel in the New Testament, who writes, 'In the beginning was the Word. The Word was with God and the Word was God.'

'Om' implies no special divine attributes and refers to no particular picture of God. It is a universal and non-specific name for the ultimate power of life, and is often used as a symbol to represent the Hindu faith. It is a natural and complete sound, the primal word – a word beyond meaning, just as God is truly an idea beyond intellectual understanding. Hindu mystics transcend the limits of the mind by meditating on this holy sound; by vibrating it repeatedly and allowing a mystical state to arise within which they merge with the mysterious oneness of God.

In Hinduism, as in many other mystical traditions, words have magical properties. It is a miracle that one person can make a sound which can convey thoughts to another, but in the modern West we have lost our reverence for words. For the ancients, to say the word 'God' was to invoke the divine presence. In our culture, words are mere tools with no significance of their own. Words like 'God' and 'spirituality' have become dead. Often we do not feel comfortable about using them, and even if we do it is without a full awareness of their profound meaning. When used with this awareness, however, they can bring to consciousness the object of their meaning. This is the basis of the mystical practice of mantra repetition.

The mystic path is the path of Love Supreme.

KABIR
Fifteenth-century Indian poet

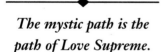

THE GURU

At the heart of all Hindu mystic paths stands the extraordinary figure of the guru. 'Guru' means 'one who leads from darkness to light'. These enlightened masters are living embodiments of the truth of their teachings. They have the power to awaken their students to the mystic knowledge that they themselves have found. The guru sees this same spiritual potential in the devotee. This knowing cannot be taught, however, but, like a lit candle lighting an unlit candle, the mystical understanding is directly transmitted from teacher to pupil. The genuine guru has transcended his separate self and so for his devotees is a pure embodiment of God. This is why the guru is often described as a perfect mirror. By devoting himself to his guru, the devotee surrenders himself to God.

Hindus believe that by simply spending time in the presence of such a being some of his insight will be absorbed by the seeker through osmosis – a practice called *darshan*. The respect and love felt by the devotee to his master is beautifully expressed by the mystic poet Kabir, who writes, 'If all the land in the world were turned to paper and all the seas turned to ink, and all the forests into pens to write with, they would still not suffice to describe the greatness of the guru.'

The spiritual essence of the true guru's message is always the same mystical philosophy. The teachers themselves, however, are far from similar. Some are regarded as avatars – incarnations of God, while others are simply seen as enlightened men and women. Some are quite conventional teachers with all the qualities commonly associated with saintliness. Others are eccentric and appear to have extraordinary lifestyles. The diversity and individuality of these great mystics can be appreciated by looking at four of the many remarkable modern Indian teachers.

GURU NANAK AND THE SIKHS

The Sikh faith originated in Pakistan and north-west India in the fifteenth century, as a synthesis of Hinduism and Islam. It started as a small group of spiritual seekers around the mystic Guru Nanak (1469–1539), who taught his followers that the aim of life was to devote oneself to dwelling on the name of God. Although Nanak is revered as a guru, he taught that the Satguru, the True Guru, is always and only God. He preached that 'There is no Hindu and there is no Muslim', and rejected both the orthodox religious priesthood and the Indian caste system. Nanak practised a mysticism of love, often describing his relationship with God as like that of a bride longing for her husband. For Nanak, God is compassionate and all-powerful. He decides all that will happen – both good and evil. He is present everywhere – 'as much in a worm as in an elephant'. By God's grace, a seeker can attain a deep inner awareness of his own nature, becoming one with God – the Satguru.

Sai Baba is the most famous and influential guru in India today. He is regarded by his devotees as an Avatar, an incarnation of the god Vishnu.

SAI BABA – MAN OF MIRACLES

To his devotees, Sathya Sai Baba is a living avatar. He is the most influential modern guru, with millions of devotees from every part of the world. His seventieth birthday celebrations in 1995 were attended by over three hundred thousand people, including a fifth of all members of the Indian Parliament. He was born of humble parents in an obscure village in southern India called Puttaparthi. As a teenager he announced that he was a reincarnation of Sai Baba of Shirdi, a respected saint who was a Muslim. When he declared his divine calling his worried family had him subjected to all sorts of spells, quackery and punishments in an attempt to make him 'normal'. Eventually they recognized that their son was indeed extraordinary, and became his devotees.

Today, Sai Baba still lives in the village of his birth and has only once left India. Puttaparthi, however, has been transformed. He has built a huge ashram where millions come to seek spiritual enlightenment. He has set up many schools, universities and hospitals, including one of the most technically advanced hospitals in Asia which provides free treatment for all regardless of wealth or status. As well as these massive practical achievements, he is well known for supernatural feats. He began performing miracles at an early age and still regularly produces from his hands holy ash called *vibuthi*, which is said to have spiritual healing powers. Thousands of people have witnessed him create talismans such as rings and jewellery from thin air.

Magical powers like these are called *siddhis*, and are well documented in India. Reports of yogis with strange abilities such as walking on water, reading others' minds, living on air alone, not needing to sleep, being able to levitate and so on are quite common. The great mystics, however, regard these powers as mere side-effects of following the mystic path, which, if used unwisely, can inflate the mystic's ego and be an impediment to reaching his true goal of self-transcendence. Sai Baba considers his miracles to be trivial. He calls them his 'calling cards', saying, 'I give people what they want, so they will want what I have to give.' What he has to give is the perennial mystical revelation of God. His miracles, which include feeding large numbers of people and raising the dead, emphasize the illusionary nature of the world which we believe is so real. His message, however, is that through love and selfless service every person can awaken his soul within and discover God. He says, 'Be your own guru; your own teacher. You have the lamp within you. Light it and march on without fear.'

◆

Love all, serve all.

SAI BABA

◆

NEEM KAROLI BABA – THE RASCAL GURU

A far less conventional guru was the enigmatic Neem Karoli Baba, who died in 1975. He was known to his devotees by the affectionate title of Maharajji. He owned nothing but a blanket, with which he wrapped himself. He gave no coherent teachings, but, simply by the power of his being, opened the hearts of those around him to the experience of God. He behaved in strange, incomprehensible ways – appearing and disappearing all over the place, and sometimes running away from devotees who had gathered to be with him. Maharajji obeyed no rules and lived an entirely spontaneous life. He regularly showed that he was not limited by his body or mind, displaying the ability to know his devotees' every thought and action. Despite this he affirmed that God did everything, saying, 'I have no powers, I don't know anything.' A devotee recalls the atmosphere that surrounded him: 'There was gossip and laughter for he loved to joke. Orders for running the ashram were given, usually in a piercing yell across the compound. Sometimes he sat in silence, absorbed in another world to which we could not follow, but bliss and joy poured down on us.'

Maharajji's best-known devotee is the American spiritual teacher Richard Alpert, to whom he gave the spiritual name Ram Dass, which means 'Servant of God'. Ram Dass had been a professor of psychology at Harvard University, but was infamously expelled for his experiments with LSD in the 1960s. These drug-induced mystical revelations set him on a spiritual search which led to India and Neem Karoli Baba. Ram Dass writes:

> *I found in Maharajji such seamless wisdom and compassion, such clarity of perception born of true freedom, and an absence of any need on his part to exploit me, that surrender came naturally and easily. I did not experience I was surrendering to another 'ego'. He was free even of being 'somebody'. When I think of Maharajji, I immediately experience a wave of love, as though I am being immersed in an ocean of love.*

Ram Dass relates a particularly moving moment with his guru. Since they first met, Maharajji had been clearly showing that he miraculously knew all of Ram Dass's thoughts and actions, whether he had witnessed them or not. One particular day, while waiting for Maharajji to come out to give *darshan*, Ram Dass began to think to himself, 'If he knows this about me, then he must also know that – and

When you see eternity in things that pass away, and infinity in finite things, then one has pure knowledge.

Bhagavad Gita

if he knows that – oh no, he knows that!' As he brought to mind everything of which he was most ashamed, Maharajji appeared. Ram Dass hid his face, too embarrassed to look at him. When at last he dared to look up, Maharajji was beaming directly down upon him with total love and acceptance. 'What a grace it would be,' thought Ram Dass at that moment, 'if I could ever love others so unconditionally.'

RAMESH BALSEKAR AND THE ENLIGHTENED TOBACCONIST

In a small but comfortable flat amongst the noise and smog of Bombay lives Ramesh Balsekar. Unlike the saintly Sai Baba with his vast numbers of devotees, and the rascal guru Neem Karoli Baba with his enigmatic ways, Ramesh is a retired bank president, golfer and elderly family man, giving teachings each day to a small gathering of some ten to twenty people. After his retirement he became the student of a poor, semi-literate guru called Sri Nisargadatta Maharaj, visiting him regularly in his home in the slums of Bombay. Sri Nisargadatta, whose name translates as 'Mr Natural', was a seller of cheap cigarettes and a lifelong smoker. He was also an enlightened master who communicated mystic philosophy with the extraordinary clarity that only comes from direct experience of the truth. Ramesh immediately recognized him as an enlightened sage and absorbed his teachings until he directly experienced their truth and, as he puts it, 'Enlightenment took place.'

Sri Nisargadatta presented the same perennial wisdom that his own guru had imparted to him, but in his own idiosyncratic way. This led his peers to complain that he was revising his master's teachings. Likewise, although completely true to the spirit of Sri Nisargadatta's philosophy, Ramesh's expression of it is spontaneous and unique to himself. This approach, which often causes confusion, is actually the hallmark of an authentic voice – a genuine teacher who has understood the eternal truth in his own way, and can represent it using fresh images and metaphors from his living understanding. This is why mysticism is the antithesis of dogmatic religion. Religion seeks to tie things down – to create a permanent and static statement of the spiritual teachings to which everyone can adhere. The mystic knows that to confine the living truth in this way is to kill it. Although mysticism is perennial wisdom, each mystic must arrive at his own unique understanding.

The Self is all-knowing, it is all-understanding, and to it belongs all glory. It is Pure Consciousness, dwelling in the hearts of all.

Mindaha Upanishad

WHO AM I?

Sri Nisargadatta and Ramesh Balsekar both teach a profound mystical path called Advaita, which was powerfully articulated by the eighth-century sage Sankara. Advaita is a very clear statement of the mystical philosophy that in one way or another underlies the experience of the great mystics of all traditions. At first it can seem strange and challenging, but when understood it is the key to demystifying mysticism. It shows that discovering the higher self is not something other-worldly, but an immediate awareness that anyone can experience right here and now. Sri Nisargadatta teaches: 'The seeker is he who is in search of himself. Give up all questions except one: "Who am I?" After all, the only fact you are sure of is that you *are*. The "I am" is certain. The "I am this" is not.'

Every moment every person is sure of one thing – that they exist. Each one of us has a sense of being, which we express in the phrase 'I am'. This is the only thing which is permanent in our lives. Our bodies grow older, our personalities change, our feelings fluctuate, our thoughts come and go – but this sense of 'I' is always with us. This awareness is the background to all experiences. The mystic shifts his attention from the foreground of transitory sensations and thoughts to this permanent background of his sense of being.

Upon close examination, however, he sees that while he can say a great deal about his body and personality, he can say nothing about

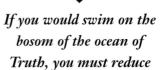

If you would swim on the bosom of the ocean of Truth, you must reduce yourself to a zero.

MAHATMA GANDHI

PARAMAHANSA YOGANANDA

Paramahansa Yogananda is widely recognized as one of the great spiritual figures of the twentieth century. His *Autobiography of a Yogi* is a mystical classic and has been translated into eighteen languages. From an early age his life was marked by miraculous encounters with Indian saints and sages. In 1920 his guru, Sri Yuketeswar Giri, sent Yogananda as an emissary to the West. Here he founded the Self-Realization Fellowship to spread his mystical teachings. Yogananda taught:

'Truth is no theory, no speculative system of philosophy, no intellectual insight. Truth is exact correspondence with reality. For man, truth is the unshakeable knowledge of his real nature, his Self.' Paramahansa Yogananda entered *mahasamadhi* – the yogi's final conscious exit from his body – in 1952 in America. The mortuary director was astonished that his body had developed no odours or other signs of decay even twenty days after death.

this sense of 'I'. It just *is*. It has no qualities. It is pure consciousness. He cannot even say it is *his* consciousness. It is *the* consciousness. This is the deepest teaching of mysticism, encapsulated by the Hindu phrase '*Atman* is Brahman' – the soul is God. All consciousness is the One Consciousness which is God. In the transcendental experience of enlightenment the mystic realizes the truth of this teaching and ceases to exist as a separate 'person'. Everything is God. There is only the all-embracing oneness.

NO SELF, NO DOER, NO THINKER

For sages such as Ramesh Balsekar, human beings are no more than 'body–mind organisms' programmed by genetics and conditioning to react in certain ways. These organisms suffer the illusion of having a personal identity, and this is the cause of all their problems. Close investigation shows that there is no 'self'; there is no 'doer' or 'thinker'. Actions are just happening in the same natural way that the sun rises and sets. Thoughts arise, but there is no thinker. They occur as organically and spontaneously as flowers grow and rain falls. Everything is happening by God's will and being witnessed by the one consciousness. Ramesh says: 'Whatever decision we think we are making is actually being made for us, because the decision is the end result of a thought and we have no control over the arising of the thought.'

The profound but ironic conclusion of Ramesh's teaching is that because there is no 'doer' nothing can be done to speed up the natural process of enlightenment. It will happen when it happens, just like everything else. Anything that the 'person' does by way of spiritual practice to achieve enlightenment can only add to the illusion of there being a 'person'. Ramesh says:

Enlightenment is merely an impersonal happening. We give it the taint of personal achievement. Therefore the question arises, 'What is an enlightened being like?' There is no such thing as an enlightened person. Enlightenment is merely another event. There is a flood, a fire, an earthquake; there is enlightenment, just one happening in the whole process, all part of the phenomenal process.

4

BUDDHIST MYSTICISM

◆

With a single stroke we are freed from bondage;
nothing clings to us and we hold to nothing.
All is empty, clear, illuminating itself
with no exertion of the mind's power.
Here thought, feeling, learning and imagination are worthless.
In this Suchness there is no 'I';
nor is there anything 'other-than-I'.

SENGSTAN
Sixth-century Zen Patriarch

The teachings of the Buddha are symbolically represented as the Dharma Chakra, *the wheel of the law.*

*T*HE BUDDHA lived in India in the fifth century BC. His teachings, based on his own direct mystical revelations, were a powerful reawakening of the spirit of experiential mysticism within Hinduism. To the priestly authorities of the day it was a dangerous individualistic heresy which challenged their power, but by the third century BC the Emperor Asoka had established it as the religion of the entire Indian empire. Hinduism, however, is fundamentally such an all-embracing religion that before long it had absorbed the Buddha back into the fold, seeing him as an avatar of the god Vishnu, and today there are more Christians in India than there are Buddhists. Buddhism spread south to Sri Lanka, to the Far East, and north to Tibet where it merged with the indigenous shamanism to become Tibetan Buddhism. In China it interacted with the oriental path of Taoism to become Chan, which developed into the famous school of Zen Buddhism in Japan. It is a profound religion, with many great mystics and a highly developed philosophy. The Pali scriptures of the southern Buddhists alone are eleven times as long as the Bible.

In the West the popular picture of Buddhism is of silently meditating, shaven-headed monks. The everyday reality, however, is as confused and superstitious as that of any other religion. A visitor to a Thai Buddhist temple today, for example, would be confronted by a scenario that would have been anathema to the Buddha. Outside the temple are street vendors surrounded by small birds trapped in little cages. Worshippers purchase these birds and release them to show their compassion and gain spiritual 'merit'; the birds, of course, are simply recaptured and recycled to the next customer. The penniless devout rub gold leaf on to giant statues of the Buddha to show their devotion and gain more 'merit'. The temple is full of the frantic rustling of yarrow sticks as the 'worshippers' consult an oracle to discover their fortune. If the prediction is good, they buy a lottery ticket just outside the temple door on the way out, and return home a dutiful Buddhist. As in all religions, the common practices are a spiritual comfort to the adherent and perform an important social function, but have little to do with the deep mystical realizations that inspired the founders of the great faiths.

This is the Daibutsu Buddha of Japan. All cultures depict the Buddha after their own fashion, but the original was Siddartha Gautama, a prince of the Shakya tribe in India. After his enlightenment he became the Buddha, literally 'The Knower'.

THE MYSTICAL TEACHINGS OF THE BUDDHA

The Buddha actually taught a radically practical path to individual enlightenment. He was born a wealthy prince in northern India, sheltered from all forms of suffering. Perhaps because of this, when he eventually discovered the existence of illness, old age and decay he was deeply motivated to find a way of escaping from such horrors. He became a rigorous ascetic for many years, before finally finding a 'middle way' between austerity and indulgence. One day he sat down to meditate under a tree and resolved not to get up until he had truly become enlightened. After seven days of intense mystical experiences he achieved enlightenment, and spent the rest of his life teaching the essential wisdom he had found – always preferring to avoid metaphysical speculation and intellectual philosophy, and returning his students to a direct perception of reality.

The Buddha saw that all of life is inevitably pervaded by suffering. He called this transitory world of change Samsara. In it everything is impermanent, including our own bodies which ultimately face decay and death. Life is a difficult and unsatisfactory experience, which he called *duhkha*. We are always wanting something we have not got, or not wanting something which we have. Even when we do get what we want, we know that things will change sooner or later and we will lose them. While most people try to put these facts to the back of their minds, and carry on the futile struggle to be permanently happy, the Buddha looked them in the face and saw a way out.

In the world of change he discovered something permanent and immortal – the 'Buddha nature' or the higher Self. 'Buddha' means 'Knower'. The Buddha nature is the 'knower' of all experiences – the 'I am' of pure consciousness. A human being suffers, the Buddha taught, because he does not experience his permanent Buddha nature, but is caught up in the illusion that he is the impermanent body and personality. Through selfish desires he is imprisoned within his self, and so within the suffering of *duhkha*. When he knows his true Self, he is liberated and full of peace, joy, happiness, love and wisdom. The Buddha advises: 'Have your higher Self as a lamp and a refuge, and no other refuge. The Self is Lord of the self.'

ENLIGHTENMENT

Nirvana means 'going out' or 'becoming cool'. It is achieved when the flames of selfish craving are extinguished. This symbol represents the state of pure consciousness that is beyond description.

Like all great mystics, the Buddha teaches: 'Transcend your personality and discover your soul.' The Buddha, however, made a further mystical discovery, known by only the greatest of mystics who have gone to the depths of the truth. This higher Self is like a flame burning away the candle of the personal self, and when the flame completely consumes the candle, burning it into light, both flame and candle no longer exist. There is neither personality nor soul – higher or lower. There is no self at all. The individual flame returns as light to the oneness of God.

The final and complete realization of this mystic truth is known as enlightenment. The Buddha called this blissful state Nirvana, which means 'to extinguish'. In this sublime mystical realization, the mystic's separate self is blown out like a candle and he knows what the Tibetans call the Clear Light of the Void – the emptiness that contains everything. He experiences his true identity as pure impersonal consciousness. When enlightenment has occurred there is no suffering, because there is no separate 'person' to suffer. In other traditions this is called mystical union with the oneness of God.

BODHISATTVAS

Tibetan Buddhism developed from a synthesis of the teachings of the Buddha, ancient Indian Tantric practices and indigenous shamanism called Bon. In the Tibetan Buddhist tradition a realized soul will, out of compassion, often choose to reincarnate over and over again to help free others from their suffering. The best known of such reincarnated masters or bodhisattvas is His Holiness the Dalai Lama, the spiritual leader of Tibet. Such great lamas, meaning 'teachers', give themselves into complete selfless service, taking the Bodhisattva Vow: 'For as long as space endures and for as long as living beings remain – until then may I too abide to dispel the misery of the world.' The soul which travels through many births and deaths is a higher form of identity. It is not the mortal body and personality, but neither is it the ineffable 'I' of pure Consciousness. As the mystic scholar Dr W. Y. Evans-Wentz writes, 'The knower itself neither incarnates nor reincarnates – it is the spectator.'

The Buddha centred himself in the still permanence of empty consciousness and became a blissful spectator watching everything come and go, including the joys and sufferings of his own body and mind. He did not reject the world, but embraced it completely. From his enlightened perspective he saw that 'Samsara is Nirvana and Nirvana is Samsara' – that the world is contained by pure consciousness, and consciousness is only experienced because of the world which it contains. The Buddha was lost neither in the transient forms of Samsara nor in the void of empty Nirvana – they were known to be one.

MEDITATION

Meditation is an important Buddhist spiritual practice to help the seeker transcend his separate self and discover his Buddha nature. When the mind is full of thoughts the emptiness of pure consciousness is obscured, so the Buddhist mystics practise meditation to still the mind. In what is called insight meditation, the practitioner is completely passive. He focuses his attention on an object of contemplation, such as the simple sensation of breathing, and becomes a silent witness. It is often mistakenly presumed that the mystic seeks to stop his thoughts, but this is the complete antithesis of the meaning of meditation. The meditator simply watches thoughts rise and fall, like clouds passing across the sky from horizon to horizon. By sitting still and focusing his attention, he simplifies his experience so that it is easier to experience the remarkable truth that he has no control over his thoughts. They come and go regardless of his will. He is not the thinker of thoughts, but the consciousness that witnesses them. He is the clear blue sky across which the clouds pass. The modern Tibetan Lama Sogyal Rinpoche says: 'The essential nature of mind is the background to the whole of life and death, like the sky, which folds the universe in its embrace.'

By witnessing thoughts, but not identifying with them as 'his', the mystic's thoughts naturally begin to settle down, like mud in water when the water is left undisturbed. The mind, like water, then becomes transparent, and the emptiness of pure consciousness is self-evident. From this emptiness the mystic sees the miracle of existence; that, as the modern Zen master Shunryu Suzuki says, 'Moment after moment, everything comes out of nothingness. This is the true joy of life.' The mystic discovers that he is consciousness itself, not doing anything, not thinking anything, not striving after anything – not even enlightenment. In the words of the Zen master Huang-po: 'To awaken suddenly to the fact that your own Mind is the Buddha, that there is nothing to be attained or a single thought to be performed, this is the Supreme Way.'

All spiritual traditions practise some form of meditation. Beyond words, concepts or doctrines, it teaches awareness of awareness.

COMPASSION

Enlightenment is not a dry and abstract knowledge, but an experience of overwhelming love and compassion. United with all things, the Buddha became all-compassionate. Love is the very nature of pure consciousness, which accepts and embraces everything. When the heart is open we transcend our limited selves and partake of our greater identity. When it is closed and empty of love, however, we experience ourselves as distinct and separate individuals. This is why the Buddhist mystics emphasize the need to nurture compassion for all beings.

This can also be achieved through a type of meditation. In the loving kindness meditation a practitioner first focuses on someone whom he finds easy to love, bringing into his awareness natural feelings of warmth and acceptance. He then brings to mind a relative stranger to whom he is indifferent and extends these positive feelings towards him also – imagining perhaps how in other circumstances he could turn out to be a close friend, or how this person is caught up in the struggles and griefs of life just as he is himself. Finally he brings to

THE YOUNG SPANISH LAMA

In 1987 a nineteen-month-old Spanish boy called Osel Hita Torres was identified as a reincarnation of a Tibetan lama, Thubten Yeshe, who had died some fourteen months before Osel was born. Lama Yeshe himself had been identified at an early age as a reincarnated Tibetan abbess. Lama Osel is the first non-Tibetan reincarnation of a lama. When Lama Yeshe died, the task of finding his reincarnation fell to his close friend Lama Zopa. In accordance with tradition Zopa consulted mediums in touch with the guiding spirits of Tibetan Buddhism, who indicated that in his next life Lama Yeshe would be a Westerner. Lama Zopa had a dream of Lama Yeshe telling him he was about to take a human form. Later he dreamed of a Western baby crawling to meet him. When Zopa met Osel he immediately recognized him as the baby from his dream.

Osel was given the traditional tests of having to choose from a selection of hand-bells and prayer-beads, and unerringly picked Lama Yeshe's. One lama, however, was sceptical and devised his own test, presenting the child with several pairs of sunglasses including Lama Yeshe's favourites. The child immediately picked up the right sunglasses and playfully banged the lama on the head with them. At his enthronement Lama Osel chewed sweets and played with a toy car.

The 'ever-watchful eyes' are a favourite image adorning many Nepalese Buddhist temples. The Buddha's eyes look in four directions and ward off any approaching evil.

mind someone who he has alienated from his heart for some reason, and allows natural kindness and forgiveness to dissolve any divisions, bringing him into a state of unconditional love.

Meditation is not a solitary, other-worldly practice. It is the deliberate cultivation of a state of awareness that can permeate all of life, bringing the mystic into the wonder of the present moment. The living Vietnamese Zen master Thich Nhat Hanh writes:

In Buddhist meditation we do not struggle for the kind of enlightenment that will happen five or ten years from now. We practise so that each moment of our lives becomes real life. And, therefore, if we meditate, we sit for sitting; we don't sit for something else. If we sit for twenty minutes, these twenty minutes should bring us joy, life. The same kind of mindfulness can be practised when we eat breakfast, or when we hold a child in our arms, or hug our mother, or our husband, or our friend.

By stilling his mind and opening his heart, the mystic transcends his isolation and discovers the interconnectedness of the whole of life. An anonymous Buddhist monk says: 'He who clings to the void and neglects compassion does not reach the highest stage. But he who practises only compassion does not gain release from the toils of his existence. He, however, who is strong in both, remains neither in Samsara nor in Nirvana.' When the mystic knows his true nature and loves all the world, he is completely enlightened.

ZEN

In 520 Bodhidharma, the twenty-eighth Indian Buddhist Patriarch, whose name means Knower of the Way, travelled to China. Buddhism was already well established in that country, but there had never been a living enlightened master. The Emperor Wu-Ti was a devout Buddhist, so when he heard of the arrival of such a great sage he invited him to his court. He inquired of Bodhidharma, 'I have built many temples, ordained many monks, built schools and hospitals. What spiritual merit have I attained?'

'None whatsoever,' replied Bodhidharma.

The Emperor was shocked and confused. 'Please tell me, then, what is the essence of Buddhism?' he asked.

'No essence at all,' said Bodhidharma.

The Emperor tried hard to be patient. 'You say everything is nothing – well, tell me who is it that is talking to me now?' he demanded.

'I do not know,' said Bodhidharma.

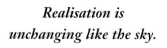

Realisation is unchanging like the sky.

**The Great Perfection
Buddhist scripture**

Enraged, the Emperor threw him out of the court.

To a country that only knew the religion of Buddhism, Bodhidharma brought the living mystical truth, but he could find no one ready to receive it. So he sat in front of a white wall in meditation for nine years until eventually a student approached him who was able to hear his ineffable message. Bodhidharma became the first Patriarch of a new school of Buddhism called Chan. Chan means 'meditation' or simply 'sitting', and it emphasizes this method of directly realizing the Truth. The thirteenth-century master Eisai took Chan to Japan, where it became known as Zen. Here it flourished, retaining Bodhidharma's uncompromising emphasis on attaining a sudden immediate perception of reality. Master Dogen, who was the pupil of Eisai, writes:

> *The burning of incense, the bowing before the Buddha's image and prayer to him, confession of sins and the reading of the Scriptures are all unnecessary. The one and only thing required is to free oneself from the bondage of mind and body alike, putting the Buddha's own seal upon yourself. If you do this as you sit in ecstatic meditation the whole universe turns into enlightenment.*

Zen students are often given a *koan* to meditate on – an impossible question which they contemplate in meditation until their mind implodes with the pressure of intense and futile mental investigation. A famous example is, 'What is your original face?' Questions like this have no logical answer, but can awaken a moment of intuitive insight beyond the rational mind. They throw the questioner back on himself until he lets go of striving to find an answer and suddenly *sees*. In this case he may perceive that, if he looks closely at his own direct experience, he has no face! This is the one thing he never sees, because this is what is doing the seeing. In the same way he may realize that he has no self, other than ineffable consciousness – the perceiver which he can never make the object of his perception.

These are only ideas, however, and cannot be an 'answer' to the *koan*. The *koan* is only answered by the mystic's direct experience. This happened to Douglas Harding, a remarkable modern English Zen mystic, who writes:

> *The best day of my life – my rebirth day so to speak – was when I found I had no head. What actually happened was something absurdly simple and unspectacular. I stopped thinking. An odd kind of limpness or numbness came upon me. Reason and imagination and all mental chatter died down. For once, words failed me. Past and future dropped away. I forgot who I was and what I was, my name, manhood, ani-*

I show the truth to living beings, and then they are no longer living beings.

TUNG SHAN
Zen master

To the man without understanding, the world is as it is. To the man with understanding, the world is as it is.

Zen Buddhist saying

malhood, all that could be called mine. It was as if I had been born that instant, brand new, mindless, innocent of all memories. There existed only the Now, that present moment and what was clearly given in it. It took me no time at all to notice that this hole where the head should have been was no ordinary vacancy, no mere nothing. On the contrary, it was very much occupied. It was a vast emptiness vastly filled, a room that found room for everything – room for grass, shadowy distant hills, and far above them snowpeaks like a row of angular clouds riding the blue sky. I had lost a head and gained the world.

MYSTICAL SUBVERSIVES

Zen is a kind of institutionalized subversion. Zen masters often deliberately undermine each other to bring the student to the realization that the Buddha is not some great master, but the seeker's own self. For example, the great sage Bodhidharma who brought Buddhism from India to the Far East is humorously described as a ridiculous figure by the thirteenth-century Zen master Mummon, who irreverently writes:

> *That broken-toothed old Hindu, Bodhidharma, came thousands of miles over the sea from India to China as if he had something wonderful. He is like raising waves without wind. After he remained years in China he had only one disciple and that one lost his arm and was deformed. Alas, ever since he has had brainless disciples. Why did Bodhidharma come to China? For years monks have discussed this. All the troubles that have followed since came from that teacher and disciple.*

Zen masters are infamous for suddenly doing something bizarre to shock their students out of their habitual minds and into a realization of the truth. The limited mind traces the same familiar routes, like a prisoner pacing up and down in his cell. But Big Mind, as the modern Zen master Shunryu Suzuki calls it, is always fresh and responsive to the present moment. When the Zen master reacts in a totally incomprehensible and unexpected way, he confronts the student's expectations. Not knowing how to react, the student is forced to respond spontaneously from his deeper being and break out of his habits. The master has released him from the prison of his preconditioned responses to life, and he is free.

Zen masters are totally identified with Nature.

D. T. SUZUKI
Zen master

In an old Zen story a student called Yamaoka Tesshu visited many masters, until at last he called on Dokuon of Shokoku. Hoping to

THE WILD WAYS OF ZEN MASTER IKKYU

The Japanese Zen master Ikkyu was born at sunrise on the first day of 1394. At the age of twenty-six, after years of arduous struggle, he was meditating in a boat when he heard the caw of a crow and was spontaneously enlightened. When his master Kaso presented him with an *inka*, a seal of enlightenment, Ikkyu threw it to the ground and walked away, saying he needed no official approval. Kaso said, 'Ikkyu is my true heir, but his ways are wild.' After the death of his master Ikkyu called himself 'a crazy cloud' and spent much of his life as a vagrant monk. He associated with artists and deeply loved poetry, himself writing exquisite Zen verse.

Ikkyu's Zen is raw, direct and authentic.

He was as much at home in a brothel as in a temple, and talks with enthusiasm about the joys of sexuality. He writes, 'A monk who loves sex, you protest! Passionate, aroused and hot-blooded. But that lust can consume all passion, transmuting base metal into pure gold.' In 1474 he became the abbot of the most important Zen temple in Japan. Not long before his death at the age of eighty-seven he told his followers, 'After I'm gone, some of you will seclude yourselves in the forests and mountains to meditate, while others may drink rice wine and enjoy the company of women. Both these kinds of Zen are fine, but if some of you become professional clerics, babbling about 'The Way of Zen', you are my enemies.'

show off his understanding of Buddhist philosophy he said, 'The mind, the Buddha and all sentient beings do not in reality exist. The true source of all phenomena is emptiness. There is no enlighten-ment, no delusion, no sage, no mediocrity. There is no giving or receiving.' Dokuon sat silently smoking his pipe and ignored the pupil, who became increasingly agitated. Suddenly Dokuon whacked Yamaoka hard with his bamboo pipe, which made him shout with anger. 'If nothing exists, where did this anger come from?' inquired Dokuon, and Yamaoka was suddenly illuminated.

A QUIET AWAKENING

Sudden mystical insight is so extraordinary that the seeker often feels he wants to rush out and tell the world about his revelation. Yet if he were to relate this to a Zen master, the master would most probably smile and tell him to ignore this ecstatic state because it will pass. The sudden mystical opening is known by the truly enlightened to be only

The Ten Bulls *are pictures used as a teaching aid in Zen Buddhism. The steps to enlightenment are pictured as a return to the primal state of innocence.*

At the seventh step the struggle to capture and control the bull, the symbol of the self, is over. The bull grazes peacefully nearby while the initiate sits at rest.

At the ninth step the initiate himself is transcended and natural harmony is restored.

a step on the way. From such heights the mystic will inevitably fall to earth: he has leapt into the air and glimpsed the view beyond the horizon, but he has not yet learnt to fly. Such freedom requires a final and complete relinquishing of the separate self, not just a burst of insight and enthusiasm.

This final enlightenment is a much quieter affair. It is not ordinary or extraordinary. It is neither important, nor insignificant. It is what it is. Things are simply seen as they are – how else could they be? No answers have been found, yet no questions remain. There is nothing to report and nothing to eulogize, just a serene and unassuming knowing. A medieval Buddhist nun wrote:

What life can compare with this? Sitting quietly by the window, I watch the leaves fall and the flowers bloom as the seasons come and go. When one reaches this stage of realisation, seeing is no-seeing, hearing is no-hearing, preaching is no-preaching. When hungry one eats, when tired one sleeps. Let the leaves fall, let the flowers bloom as they like. When the leaves fall I know it is autumn; when the flowers bloom, I know it is spring.

Seeing is no-seeing, because there is no separate self who is the seer; seeing is simply taking place. The enlightened mystic intuitively responds to the prompting of nature uncluttered by unnecessary mental processes, and, just like a little child, when hungry he eats and when tired he sleeps. Like a flower which grows and blooms and dies, he lives his life as an organic part of the natural way of things.

If the great mystics are to be believed, this natural and complete awakening is happening to men and women all the time; but such genuinely enlightened beings, by their very nature, go unnoticed. They live ordinary lives amongst ordinary folk. They are unremarkable, for they have no need to impress or seek approval. They have no opinions of their own, and so are unconcerned with the opinions of others. Yet, just by being the way they are, they transform all those around them. As it says in the Zen scripture:

Barefoot and naked of breast, I mingle with the people of the world.
My clothes are ragged and dust-laden and I am ever blissful.
I use no magic to extend my life.
Now, before me, the trees become divine.
I go to the market place with my wine bottle,
And return home with my staff.
I visit the wine shop and the market
And everyone I look upon becomes enlightened.

5

TAOIST MYSTICISM

◆

You can't see it, because it has no form.
You can't hear it, because it makes no noise.
You can't touch it, because it has no substance.
It cannot be known in these ways,
because it is the all-embracing Oneness.
It is not high and light,
or low and dark.
Indefinable yet continually present,
it is nothing at all.
It is the formless form,
the imageless image.
It can't be grasped by the imagination.
It has no beginning and no end.

This is the essence of Tao.
Stay in harmony with this ancient presence,
and you will know the fullness of each present moment.

LAO TZU
Fifth-century BC Taoist sage

The Yin-Yang motif is a dynamic symbol of life representing the resolution of all opposites and the reconciliation of all paradoxes.

THE TAOIST religion developed from ancient shamanic practices and places great importance on a life lived in accordance with nature. Today, popular Taoism is a religion full of superstition and ritual. People sleep with the works of the great sage Lao Tzu under their bed to bring them luck, rather than reading them and following his teachings. The great Taoists, however, have been extraordinary mystics with a penetrating insight into the fundamental truths of life. All of these masters look to the teachings of Lao Tzu as a sublime source of inspiration.

Lao Tzu was a contemporary of the Buddha. His name simply means 'Old Master', and he was the court librarian of the Chou state of China. One day, weary of the ways of men, he set off on an ox towards the west. Reaching the pass in the mountains at Han-ku, he stopped for the night. The gatekeeper with whom he stayed recognized the great sage who was his guest and, realizing that he would never be seen again, begged him to write down his wisdom. So Lao Tzu wrote the eighty-one aphorisms that make up the *Tao Te Ching*, which contain the central teachings of Taoism.

The mystic Lao Tzu lived at the same time as the great Chinese moralist K'ung Fu Tzu (Confucius). Unlike K'ung Fu Tzu, Lao Tzu was unconcerned with right and wrong ways to behave and the intricacies of religious rituals. He taught that it was possible to become completely natural and spontaneously act well from a deep innate goodness. It is said that K'ung Fu Tzu once paid him a visit. The historian Ssu Ma Ch'ien records that Lao Tzu said to him, 'Stop being so arrogant: all these demands; your self-importance and over-keen enthusiasms – none of this is true to yourself. That is all I have to say to you.'

K'ung Fu Tzu left, saying to his followers, 'I know that birds can fly; that fishes can swim; that animals can run. Things that run can be caught in nets. Those that fly can be shot down with arrows. But what to do with the dragon I do not know. It rises on the clouds and the wind. I have met Lao Tzu and he is like the dragon.'

THE WISDOM OF TAOISM

Lao Tzu brought new depth to the ancient Chinese spiritual philosophy of the Tao. Tao is a Chinese word meaning 'way' or 'road', and Taoism is 'The Way' – the spiritual path. Lao Tzu's usage of the word, however, has deeper mystical connotations. Tao is the way things are; the way life works; the harmony of life; the natural process of becoming. Sometimes Lao Tzu uses the word in an even more abstract way. Tao is the all and nothing; pure consciousness; the emptiness that is full of everything. It is the same supreme oneness of which all the mystics speak, using different names. Tao is the Brahman of the Hindus, the Nirvana of the Buddhists, the ineffable Godhead of the Jews, Christians and Muslims. Lao Tzu wrote: 'Mysteriously existing before Heaven and Earth. Silent and empty. An unchanging Oneness. An ever-Changing presence. The Mother of all Life. It is impossible to really give it name, but I call it "Tao".'

Taoism teaches the simple way of nature. Followers of the Tao, like the monk pictured here, practise humility and patience to become like soft water that wears away the hardest rock.

Taoism is sometimes called the way of water, because it teaches that we should not resist life, but, like water, flow around obstacles. Water is the softest thing in the world, yet it has the power to wear away hard rocks. In the same way, the Taoist mystics approach life with the power of acceptance and perseverance rather than effort and force. Just like a river rushing to the sea, the Taoists see themselves as being on a journey back to the source of the Tao. Rivers flow to the sea because it lies below them. Learning from this, the mystic who wishes to become the Tao humbly places himself below all others.

The Taoist sage becomes part of the natural flow of the universe. The fourth-century Taoist T'ao Ch'ien wrote: 'Just surrender to the cycle of things. Give yourselves to the wave of the Great Change. Neither happy nor afraid. And when it is time to go, then simply go – without any unnecessary fuss.' The Taoist mystics seek to transcend their separate identities, and know themselves to be a natural part of the Tao. Lao Tzu advises: 'Shut up! Look inside! Soften your sharp edges. Simplify your thoughts. Follow your own light. Be ordinary. Then you will see for yourself that you are a part of the Whole.'

CHUANG TZU'S DREAM

The great fourth-century BC sage Chuang Tzu, a follower of Lao Tzu, relates once having a vivid dream in which he was a butterfly. When he awoke he was puzzled. Was he a man who had dreamt he was a butterfly, or a butterfly dreaming it was a man? This story has

> *Fools regard themselves*
> *as already awake.*
>
> CHUANG TZU

many deep resonances. The butterfly is a ubiquitous symbol for the soul. We still have it in our word 'psyche', the ancient Greek word for 'soul', which also means 'butterfly'. It is an image that represents the higher Self, which is trapped in the body like a caterpillar in a chrysalis and will emerge transformed – free to fly like a beautiful winged butterfly. Chuang Tzu's question is profound. Is he a sleeping soul or a wakeful person? What is his true identity? He cannot be sure which he is – only *that he is*. His only permanent and undoubtable identity is neither as a soul nor as a person, but as pure consciousness witnessing life unfold.

The complete realization of this mystical truth is oneness with the Tao. Lao Tzu wrote: 'Be empty. Be still. Watch everything just come and go. Emerging from the Source – returning to the Source. This is the way of Nature. Be at peace. Be aware of the Source. This is the fulfilment of your destiny. Know that which never changes. This is enlightenment.'

WU WEI – NO DOER

The I Ching *or Book of* Changes *is an ancient Chinese system of divination now becoming popular in the West. The eight 'trigrams' pictured here are combined to produce 64 'hexagrams' of six lines each. Obtaining one such hexagram by throwing coins leads to the relevant chapter of the* I Ching *whose answers are both simple and profound.*

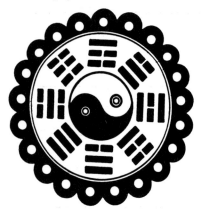

Knowing that there is no separate self, only consciousness witnessing life unfolding, the sage is in a state of *wu wei*. This phrase is the most misunderstood of all Taoist concepts. Its literal translation is 'not doing', which is often mistakenly interpreted as a form of quietism. The sage is pictured as withdrawing from life so that he may avoid interfering with the flow of things by remaining inactive. The Taoist sages, however, are full of life and very much in the world. The *Tao Te Ching*, for example, is as much about statecraft as it is about meditation and philosophy. The sage who experiences *wu wei* is not inactive – there is simply no 'actor'. He has seen through all separateness and identified with the pure consciousness of Tao. Actions happen, but there is no 'person' performing them. Thoughts arise, but there is no 'thinker' who thinks them. *Wu wei* is better translated as 'no doer'. Taoism is called 'The Natural Way' because for the sage there is no separate self interfering with the natural organic process that is life. Lao Tzu wrote: 'The wise know there is no one to go anywhere. There is seeing, but no one looking. Doing naturally arises from Being.'

Chuang Tzu tells the story of a one-legged dragon called Hui, who asks a centipede, 'How do you manage all those legs? I can hardly manage one.'

The centipede replies, 'As a matter of fact, I do not manage my legs.'

The centipede lets his legs manage themselves. The sage allows all of life to manage itself naturally. We all allow basic bodily functions such as digestion to occur without 'doing' them. If we had to think about them, it would be a great burden. The sage who has merged with Tao allows his personality to function just by itself. All our human sufferings are the result of assuming the unnecessary burden of trying to manage our lives, instead of allowing things simply to be what they are.

TAI CHI CHUAN

Every morning the parks of China and Hong Kong are filled with a most peculiar sight. People of all ages, shapes and sizes assemble and move their bodies as if performing a beautiful, mysterious, stately dance in slow motion or under water. The air seems to have become dense and resistant, needing concentration and effort to move through it. Yet the faces of these people show no sign of strain or stress. Each limb seems loose, and an aura of gentle calmness pervades their movements. Every strange position that their bodies create flows naturally into the next, like water tumbling down a hillside. Yet they seem solid and balanced, like old trees rooted deep into the ground.

These people are practising Tai Chi Chuan, sometimes called Chinese yoga. 'Tai Chi' means 'Supreme Ultimate' and, as well as being a martial art, it is a spiritual path whose goal is achieving Oneness with the Tao. Whereas Indian yoga works through stretching and holding postures, Tai Chi Chuan emphasizes relaxation and constant movement. Like the ancient Chinese wisdom found in the *I Ching* or *Book of Changes*, Tai Chi Chuan masters teach that everything is in constant flux and that to stay in harmony with ourselves and our surroundings we must learn the art of harmonious change.

THE SAGE

The great sages who experienced the state of *wu wei* achieved a state of sublime indifference. As Chuang Tzu wrote: 'Oblivious of their own existence, they made no plans, therefore failing they had no cause of regret or succeeding no cause of congratulations. They cheerfully played their allotted parts, waiting patiently for the end.'

The sage has no sense of a personal 'I'. He is completely identified with nature. He is spontaneous like a little child. He is as simple and

To know Tao is the most wonderful thing in the world.

LAO TZU

natural as an uncarved block of wood. He is a passive vehicle of Tao. He knows he knows nothing, because he is nothing. He feels no anger, guilt or blame. He passes through life untouched by changing fortunes or by the displeasure of others. Chuang Tzu suggests we think of ourselves as being in a boat on a river, and another empty boat collides with us. Even an irritable person, he remarks, would not lose their temper. But suppose there was someone in the second boat. Then we would shout to him to keep clear, and if he did not listen the first time, nor even when we called three times, a row would certainly ensue. In the first case there was no anger but in the second there was, because in the first case the boat was empty and in the second it was occupied. 'And so it is with man,' says Chuang Tzu. 'If he could only pass empty through life, who would be able to injure him?'

The twentieth-century psychologist and mystic Carl Jung, who was highly influenced by Taoism, conveyed the natural state of *wu wei* when he wrote in his autobiography:

When people say I am wise, or a sage, I cannot accept it. A man once lifted a hatful of water from a stream. What did that amount to? I am not the stream. I am at the stream, but I do nothing. Other people are at the stream, but most of them find they have to do something with it. I do nothing. I never think that I am the one who must see to it that cherries grow on stalks. I stand and behold, admiring what nature can do.

OPPOSITE: *Buddha, Lao-Tzu and Confucious were all Eastern sages who appeared in the sixth century BC. They are pictured here together although there is no evidence that they actually met.*

OVERLEAF: *'The School of Athens' by Raphael depicts well known figures of the Italian Rennaissance as the great pagan sages. Zoroaster, Pythagoras and Diogenes are all shown, and here Leonardo da Vinci is pictured as the Greek sage Plato.*

三聖圖

6

THE MYSTERY SCHOOLS

◆

Then the High Priest
ordered all uninitiated people to depart,
and led me by the hand
into the inner recesses of the sanctuary itself.
I have no doubt, curious reader,
that you are eager to know
what happened when I entered . . .
I will say as much as I may to the uninitiated,
but only on the condition that you believe me.
I approached the very gates of death,
yet was permitted to return . . .
At midnight I saw the sun shining as if it were noon;
I entered the presence of the gods of the underworld
and the gods of the upperworld
and worshipped them.
Well, now you have heard what happened,
but I fear you are still none the wiser.

LUCIUS APULEIUS
Second-century initiate

The Mystery Schools of Crete pictured incarnation as the entrance to a dark labyrinth. The myth of the minotaur contains encoded secret teachings.

OPPOSITE: *The Pythagoreans were a mystical sect of ancient Greece. They worshipped numbers as The Immortal Gods and brought Babylonian and Egyptian knowledge to the West.*

*A*T THE SAME TIME as the Taoist sage Lao Tzu was reinvigorating Taoism in China, and the Buddha was transforming Hinduism in India, the great Greek sage Pythagoras was refining the mystical wisdom of the ancient Mystery Schools with teachings that he brought from the East. The Mystery Schools of ancient Greece and Egypt form the major inspiration for all subsequent Western mysticism, and are the foundation of our modern culture. They are the birthplace of science and mathematics, rational philosophy, the Olympic Games, and arts such as theatre and music. These activities are now all regarded as secular and little to do with spirituality, but they all grew from the fertile soil of ancient mysticism.

These schools were great mystic universities for the study of the mysteries of life and death. The most famous thinkers, artists and statesmen of the ancient Western world – people who excelled at abstract science, who created exquisite works of art, who assembled the first libraries, who built the mighty Pyramids and the Parthenon – were all mystic initiates who held the sacred mysteries to be the height of their culture. The ancient Egyptian Mystery Schools were venerated by the Greeks for their antiquity, and the Greek Mysteries in turn were held in high esteem by the Romans. The first-century BC Roman initiate Cicero enthused: 'These Mysteries have brought us from rustic savagery to a cultivated and refined civilisation … The rites of the Mystery Schools are called "initiations" and in truth we have learned from them the first principles of life. We have gained the understanding not only to live happily but also to die with better hope.'

These sacred universities were a product of indigenous religious beliefs which had developed from primal shamanic roots, and from the spiritual influence of India with whom the ancient West was in regular contact. The incense burnt in Greek temples was usually sandalwood, and a popular food was rice, both imported from India, along with Eastern mystical ideas and practices. Many great Greek sages were said to have visited India and been influenced by the profound spirituality they found there. The semi-mythical figure of Orpheus, the founder of the Orphic Mystery School, may indeed have been an Indian. By the third century BC there were even Buddhist monasteries in the Greek colonial city of Alexandria in Egypt, and a shrine in Athens to a Buddhist monk who had set himself on fire to protest at Alexander's invasion of India.

The Mystery Schools revealed through direct experience the perennial mystic teaching that life is a journey of spiritual awakening; a process by which humans may find their higher nature and become what the ancients called 'gods'. The pagan mystics taught that each individual is a spark of the one fire of life, as represented by the sun. The name of the Greek Sun God, Apollo, means 'not many', and the mystic path was seen as a journey with the aim of finding, within the multiplicity of things, the underlying oneness of God. The initiate Plotinus described someone who experiences such a realization:

> *He has attained to the oneness of untroubled stillness; undistracted and unbusied with his self, he is utterly at rest. He is no longer attracted by beautiful things, but has gone beyond attraction; surpassing even virtue. He is like someone who enters the inner sanctuary, leaving behind the temple statues. In that holy place, his relationship is not with a statue, but with Godhead itself. And this is not an object of vision, but another mode of seeing; a detachment from self; a simplification and surrender of self; a yearning for contact; a stillness and meditation directed towards transformation. Only in this way can someone behold what lies within the sanctuary. For one who looks otherwise, there is nothing to be seen.*

THE MASK OF THE 'PERSONA'

Our word 'personality' comes from the ancient term *persona*, meaning a mask used during ritual drama in the Mystery Schools. The secret imparted to the initiate in these mystical rites was that the 'personality' was no more than a mask, and behind this mask lay his soul – his 'higher Self' which the ancients called the 'genius'. This higher self is presently imprisoned within the physical body, which is no more than a shadow of this true Self. From the point of view of the personality, the genius is experienced as a separate being – a guiding angel or inner guru. As the Greek philosopher Plato said, 'We should think of the most authoritative part of our soul as a guardian spirit given by God, which lifts us from the earth towards our home in heaven.'

A similar message is conveyed in the *Odyssey*, written by Homer in the ninth century BC. In this epic poem, the adventurer Odysseus is surprised to see the great hero Heracles in hell. His guide explains to him, however, that whilst Heracles' shadow is here in Hades, Heracles

> *Our Soul has to be at the moment of death as it is during the Mysteries – free from any blemish, passion, envy or anger.*
>
> **PORPHYRY**
> **Third-century Syrian initiate**

himself is where he always is – at a banquet with the gods. In Greek literature, the journey to the underworld is a metaphor for the soul's descent into this physical world. Here it lives as a shadow of its true Self, which is always with God.

The mystic realizes that he is more than mortal flesh and blood. He is himself an eternal 'god' – a divine being. 'Do you not know that you are gods?' asks Cicero. 'Men are immortal gods – gods mortal men,' says the initiate Heraclitus. This is the great mystical revelation, a discovery that is accompanied by joy and relief – for the mystic is thus liberated from the illusion that he is only a body which is destined to age and die. He is now secure in the knowledge that, whatever twists and turns his life may take and whatever challenges and suffering he must confront, his transcendental soul remains untouched by the vicissitudes of this impermanent world.

ESCAPING THE WHEEL OF GRIEF

The ancient mystics believed that on its spiritual journey each soul passes through many lives in a recurring circle of birth, death and rebirth. Pythagoras called this 'the Grievous Wheel'. It was also known as the Wheel of Necessity, meaning 'never ceasing' – the spinning wheel on which, according to Greek mythology, the fates spun the destiny of every person. The ancients saw this wheel pictured in the stars as the zodiac, whose cycles mirror and foretell the fate that lies in wait for each of us. The image of an ever-turning wheel of change is ubiquitous. The Hindus talk of the Wheel of Karma – the cycle of cause and effect which produces our future inevitably from our past actions. The Buddha spoke of the Wheel of Suffering. The path of the mystics is to escape this Grievous Wheel. The gravestone of a fourth-century BC initiate is inscribed:

> *I have flown out of the sorrowful, weary wheel.*
> *Like a young goat I have fallen into milk.*

Pythagoras spent twenty years being initiated into the Mystery Schools of Egypt – a tradition so ancient that the Greeks looked on it with veneration. The Great Pyramid at Giza was the setting for ritual initiation of death and rebirth in the Egyptian Mysteries. These amazing edifices were more than just tombs: the construction of the

Pyramids represented the two ways open to the soul. From the King's Chamber at the centre of the Pyramid there are two thin shafts which reach through the stone and precisely align to specific stars. At the time of their construction the south shaft gave a view of the zodiac, representing the ever-turning Wheel of Grief. The other shaft revealed the northern polar star, which appears in the heavens as a fixed and unmoving point and so represented the eternally static centre of the wheel. The only escape from the wheel was for the soul to become one with the still point at the centre, and this is the mystic's quest. To do so he must abandon his self, for if the centre has any size it too will spin. The still point is a dimensionless dot – the nothing at the centre of everything.

> *We are imprisoned within a body, like an oyster within a shell.*
>
> **PLATO**

THE MYSTICAL PRACTICES OF THE MYSTERY SCHOOLS

The students of the Mystery Schools underwent many years of spiritual training. The Lesser Mysteries were open to all and included religious festivals, worship of the gods and sacred plays. The Greater Mysteries, however, were a profound secret that could only be entered by personal initiation after an inner calling by the goddess. To enter these Greater Mysteries without such a genuine calling or to reveal their secrets to the uninitiated would be to court untold personal misfortune. The Greater Mysteries were of such power and held in such respect that they were never written down. It is possible, however, to reconstruct much of these profound teachings from the many hints and clues that have been left for us.

The first step in preparation for initiation was to become a *mystae* – a word that is the root of our words 'mystery' and 'mysticism'. *Mystae* means literally 'eyes closed'. As the name suggests, the *mystae* were learning to look inside through contemplation and meditation. They were called the 'hearers', and some took a vow of silence during their five years of initial spiritual training. The *mystae* purified themselves by publicly confessing all their failings and misdeeds. This was not an empty formality, but a truly pious act. The despotic Roman Emperor Nero turned back from seeking initiation into the Greek Mysteries when he realized he would have to admit to having murdered his mother. He accepted this loss of face, rather than lie before the most sacred institution of the ancient world.

The *mystae* also underwent purification through baptism and ritual washing. They dressed in white and ate a vegetarian diet. The

The masons of the middle ages kept alive the Pythagorean wisdom. Over the south door of Chartres cathedral in France they carved his likeness as a tribute to the master-builder.

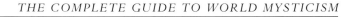

The downward pointing torch of the Goddess Demeter indicates the underworld journey that awiats the veiled initiate. Her gaze and right foot point to the threshold of an inner sanctum.

Mysteries were said to 'erase all taint where meat had been', and never involved animal sacrifice. The body was honoured as the temple of the soul. Every sacred sanctuary had a stadium for physical games and bodily development. These are the origins of the Olympic Games, named after Mount Olympus, the spiritual home of the gods. We now think of sport as an entirely profane activity, but its birthplace is in the sacred Mysteries. Runners at Delphi, for instance, ran on a track of nine lanes in honour of the nine muses – the goddesses who inspire all human accomplishments, including music, which bears their name to this day. Many athletes are familiar with the altered states of awareness that pushing the body to new heights of achievement can inspire. Within the Mystery Schools, this was acknowledged as a kind of mystical yoga.

The *mystae* purified the mind through the study of mathematics and geometry. This too was a sacred, not secular, pursuit. To discover the secrets of numbers, and how they manifested in the natural world, was to look into the very mind of God. Numbers are the fundamental building blocks of life; Pythagoras called them 'immortal gods'. Over the sacred Academy of the great philosopher Plato were written the words: 'Let no man who knows no mathematics enter here.' An understanding of the subject was the basis of ancient science. We now think of science as the antithesis of mysticism, but to the ancients the two were the same thing. They are both ways of discovering the secrets of life. To study creation is to know the Creator.

The extent of the scientific knowledge acquired by the initiates of the Mystery Schools is exemplified by some of the five hundred thousand books contained within the great pagan library of Alexandria. On these shelves stood books by famous thinkers whose ideas would dominate the sciences until the late Middle Ages: Euclid, who systemized geometry; Archimedes and Ptolemy, who did the same for physics and geography; the astronomer Aristarchus of Samos, who argued that the stars are a huge distance away and that the Earth is one of the planets and like them orbits the sun; Eratosthenes, who knew that the Earth was round and calculated its circumference to within a few per cent. There was even a book called *Automata* by Heron of Alexandria – its subject was robots.

THE HERO'S PATH

The Greek word 'catharsis' means 'purification', and the *mystae* were also purified by undergoing cathartic transformation through the spectacle of tragic drama which retold sacred myths. The great mys-

All those who participated in the Mysteries led an innocent, calm and holy life. They died looking for the light of the heavenly Elysian Fields.

**ARISTOPHANES
Fourth-century BC
Greek dramatist**

MYSTERY SCHOOL FESTIVALS

The Festival of the Mysteries in Athens lasted nine days, beginning with the inhabitants dancing along the Sacred Way to the sanctuary of Eleusis. Here they watched sacred dramas that lasted from nightfall until sunrise, were baptised in the sea and drank psychedelic ambrosia. The chosen were then initiated into the Mysteries. The women's festival, called Thesmorphia, was the one week of the year in which women were allowed out of the home unaccompanied. They went up into wooded hills where they performed the rites of the god Dionysus, singing and dancing themselves into wild, ecstatic states. It was rumoured that at the heights of their celebrations they tore to pieces a young goat, or even a young child. Men were strictly forbidden to attend. A play called *The Bacchae* by Euripides tells the story of a king who goes to spy on the women's festival. Dionysus puts a spell on the king's mother, who sees him but, mistaking him for a lion cub, decapitates him and walks back to Athens with his head on a stick.

tic playwright Sophocles likened the purging of emotions experienced while watching such plays to the process of initiation itself. Every sacred site in ancient Greece had its own theatre for this purpose. Through myth, the sages of the Mystery Schools encoded their mystic teachings into stories. The Twelve Trials of the Hero, for example, are parables to guide the soul through the tests and tribulations of life. The hero is identified with the sun, and his progress is symbolically represented by the sun passing through the twelve signs of the zodiac. The hero is 'everyman', and his journey is the journey made by all of us. The trials of the hero's path are symbols of the obstacles that each soul must face and overcome.

The Twelve Trials of Heracles, for instance, include a journey to the underworld to bring back the triple-headed hound of hell. The descent to the underworld symbolically represents the incarnation of the soul into a human life. The triple-headed hound of hell is a symbol of time – past, present and future. The first of the monster's heads is that of a wolf, which, like the past, drags its prey away into the darkness. The second is that of a lion, which, like the present, leaps upon its victim in one awful second. The third is that of a dog, which forlornly looks up to its master in the same way that we look to the future with desperate hope of better things to come. This myth teaches that the hero must overcome time if he is to find the eternal oneness of God and escape the Grievous Wheel.

The hieroglyphs of ancient Egypt remained undeciphered until the 18th century. The winged sun, (see above), *the Ankh or key of life, and the knot of eternity adorn every tomb and temple in Egypt.*

The trials of Heracles are not all macho adventures. To be whole, he must also discover his feminine side. One of his tests is to dress as a woman and learn to spin and sew. Only by balancing his masculine and feminine natures can he embody Hermes, the god of knowledge, and Aphrodite, the goddess of love, and become Hermaphrodite – a whole person. The Mystery Schools taught the mystic to use both his head and his heart in his search for the oneness in which all dualities come together.

SEEING THE SUN AT MIDNIGHT

The final and most important element of the Mystery Schools was the experience of initiation, through which the pagan mystics directly experienced the transcendent supreme reality. Lucius Apuleius tries to capture the ineffable and paradoxical nature of this revelation by saying that he 'saw the sun at midnight' – a phrase not dissimilar to the Tibetan Buddhists' encounter with the Clear Light of the Void.

During his initiation, the mystic beheld the divine light of God, within which he saw visions of the gods and goddesses who guided him on his mystic journey. The fourth-century Platonist philosopher Proclus writes: 'In the Mysteries the gods reveal many forms of themselves. They come from Light, sometimes formless, sometimes in human shape, or transmuted into other forms.' The Greek initiate Aristides records: 'There came from the Goddess Isis a Light, and other things beyond understanding, to further my salvation.' The Roman historian Plutarch reverently exclaims, 'On seeing the great light the initiate will assume another character and maintain silence and awe will hold him.' Plato talks of 'beauty shining in brightness', saying, 'We beheld the beatific vision and were initiated into the Mystery which may truly be called blessed, celebrated by us in a state of innocence ... We beheld calm, happy, simple, eternal visions, resplendent in pure light.'

Mystics who followed the Egyptian goddess Isis practised their own secret Mysteries, culminating in naked baptism in the sea at midnight under a full moon. It was after such a baptism that Lucius Apuleius had this extraordinary vision of Isis:

An apparition of a woman began to rise from the sea with a face so lovely that the gods themselves would have fallen down in adoration. Her whole body shimmered, poised on the surface of the waves ... Her long thick hair fell in ringlets on her beautiful neck, woven with every kind of flower. Above her brow shone a round disc like a mirror or the bright face of the moon. In her left hand she held vipers . . . Her many-coloured robes of the finest linen glistened crocus-yellow and glowing-red . . . But what caught my eye the most was the deep black lustre of her mantle . . . It was embroidered with glittering stars on the hem, and in the middle beamed a full and fiery moon . . . All the perfumes of Arabia filled my sense as the Goddess addressed me: 'I am Nature, the Universal Mother . . . Although I am worshipped in many aspects and known by many names, the whole round Earth venerates me.'

> **Man as he now is has ceased to be the All. But when he ceases to be an individual, he raises himself again and penetrates the world.**
>
> **PLOTINUS**

RITUAL DEATH

To be reborn in spirit the initiate underwent a ritual death which forced him to disidentify with his mortal body and personality and awakened his immortal soul. In the rites of the Great Mother, the initiates were buried in a great trench and known as 'those about to die'. Apuleius describes himself as undergoing a 'voluntary death'. Proclus describes the Dionysiac–Orphic rites, initiations under the patronage of the gods Dionysus and Orpheus, saying, 'In the most secret of initiations, the priests command that the body should be completely buried except the head.'

These initiations took place at midnight and, like ancient shamanic practices, would have been quite terrifying affairs. The Christian monk known as Pseudo-Dionysius, who was also a pagan initiate, affirms: 'The Mysteries are delivered in allegories to strike terror and awe.' Such extreme methods directly confront the mystic with the fact of his mortality, and in so doing he is forced to let go of his limited personal ego and discover that he is a spark of immortal God. Proclus says that, as a result of such a powerful initiation, 'the Spirit in us is known to be Divine – the very image of God.'

Death itself was seen as the supreme initiation. Plato says, 'To die is to be initiated.' Plutarch writes, 'The highest of our initiations in this world is only a dream of that true vision and initiation, and the Mysteries have been carefully conceived to awaken memories of the sublime things to come.' He directly compares the experience of dying and mystic initiation:

In death the Soul undergoes an experience like that of those receiving initiation into the great Mysteries. First of all, wandering painful tortuous ways, peering uneasily into the endless darkness. Then frightful

THE RENAISSANCE – THE REBIRTH OF PAGANISM

The arrival in fourteenth-century Florence of ancient pagan manuscripts by sages such as Plato, Plotinus and Hermes inspired a rebirth of ancient pagan mysticism. Great men including Leonardo da Vinci, Marsilio Ficino, Michelangelo, Raphael and Botticelli were all deeply influenced by a new Platonic Academy set up in Florence, in which the participants studied the ancient Mysteries and venerated the pagan gods so often portrayed in the paintings of this period. Such pictures were much more than decorations. Botticelli's *Birth of Venus*, for example, was painted at a precise astrological moment as a 'talisman of occult radiance', capable of magically transporting the viewer to an altered state of spiritual awareness. Raphael portrayed the members of the New Florentine Academy as the great ancient pagan sages – Heraclitus, Zoroaster, Diogenes, Socrates, Aristotle and so on. At the centre, dressed as Plato, stood Leonardo. The rediscovery of ancient mysticism in Florence led to an extraordinary flowering of arts and science known as the Renaissance, meaning 'rebirth', which laid the foundation for our modern age.

fear, terrors, sweats and stupor. After this the Soul beholds a marvellous light and is received into pure places, with beautiful meadows and voices, choral singing, dancing, and the most solemn sacred sounds and holy sights. Amid this the man, now perfect and initiated, is free, liberated, crowned. He performs the holy rites and consorts with pure men in bliss.

What occurred in these initiations that inspired such extraordinary mystical visions? In some sacred setting, as the culmination of years of preparation, the initiates of the Mystery Schools experienced a profound shift in consciousness that transported them beyond their normal awareness, revealing divine wonders. Something happened that left them awe-struck and transformed – changed and grateful beyond measure. Lucius Apuleius says of this moment of mystical rebirth, 'That was the happiest day of my initiation, and I celebrate it as a birthday . . . I remained for some days longer in the temple, enjoying the ineffable pleasure of contemplating the Goddess's statue, because I was bound to her by a debt of gratitude so large that I could never hope to repay it.'

7

JEWISH MYSTICISM

Soul, yearning soul, soul of power and of dream!
Soul that would preserve and yet lose itself!
Soul that desires everything.
Both duration and Eternity; meaning and mystery.
Here is the boundary.
Here is the altar of the world.
No one goes beyond here unless he sacrifices his self.
For this place is named 'The Choice of God'.
Up to here this and that hold good.
But here is the beginning of Unity.

BAAL SHEM
Eighteenth-century Hasidic mystic

The Menorah, or seven branched candlestick, is a feature of every Jewish home and synagogue. It is lit at the festival of the Passover which celebrates the Jews delivery from bondage in Egypt.

T**HE RICHNESS** and fertility of the Jewish mystical imagination has been the soil from which have grown three great religions – Judaism, Christianity and Islam. Jesus, of course, was a Jew, and Muhammad was greatly influenced by the Jewish communities near Mecca. The Arabs, like the Jews, traced their ancestry back to Abraham. All these religions are monotheistic – they believe in one God and reject the idea of many gods and goddesses. On the face of it, this would seem to be more in keeping with the mystic's vision of the Supreme Oneness. However, the God pictured by monotheistic religious orthodoxy is not the sublime impersonal one God of the mystics.

In the polytheistic faiths there is an ultimate faceless divinity who has no attributes apart from being, and many gods and goddess who express different attributes of this divinity. The monotheism that developed in and from Judaism banished all of these masks of God – not in favour of unmasking God, but by insisting upon one particular mask. Yahweh (Jehovah), the God of the Old Testament, was seen as having a personality with particular characteristics – he is jealous, angry, partisan, fearful, just and sometimes compassionate. This is because to the early Israelites, Yahweh was originally a tribal war-god, worshipped along with many others. When the early Jews made Yahweh the one and only god, they did not move from a belief in many gods to one *universal* God, but to one *particular* god in opposition to all others. This has been the major reason for monotheism's intolerance of other faiths, as well as its suspicion and persecution of mystics. This can be seen particularly in the history of Christianity and Islam.

Despite this, the mystics have sought the perennial vision of the supreme impersonal one God, drawing on the best in their own traditions and supplementing it with philosophy and practices inherited from mystics of other spiritual traditions. The Jewish mystics compensated for the lack of gods and goddesses by developing a complex system of different names for God to represent the supreme divinity's many aspects. In the Middle Ages, this practice gave birth to the great flowering of Jewish mysticism known as Kabbala. This in turn was the foundation of a later explosion of a more devotional Jewish mysticism in eighteenth-century Poland known as Hasidism. These are the high points of Jewish mysticism, and both paths are still followed today.

Kabbala has also had a profound impact on other traditions. It became central to the western occult tradition, sometimes called magic, that developed from the ancient Mystery Schools, and is much in evidence today in the modern New Age movement.

OLD TESTAMENT MYSTICISM

Judaism is rooted in the great mystical visions of the Old Testament prophets, which are often awesomely dramatic. The prophet Jacob met an angel with whom he wrestled, demanding that it reveal its name to him. The mystics interpreted this as a spiritual analogy of the struggle to find the higher Self. The angel finally yielded and revealed its true identity as none other than God, just as the individual consciousness of the soul is eventually realized by the mystic to be a part of the one consciousness of God. After this experience, Jacob was known as 'God-wrestler'. He is also famous for his great dream of a ladder connecting heaven and earth, on which angels passed up and down. This image became central to Jewish mystical practices in which the mystic seeks to ascend Jacob's ladder, each rung of which is an attribute of God, until he reaches the one God – 'I am'.

The Star of David, or Seal of Solomon, is an ancient Jewish symbol. The downward triangle of spirit intersects with the upward aspiration of matter.

Moses experienced God as fire in a vision on the summit of holy Mount Sinai and returned bearing the ten commandments, his face so radiant that the Israelites shrank from coming near him. In Moses' vision God names himself 'Ehyeh-Asher-Ehyeh', which means 'I am that I am'. To the Jewish mystics this is the ineffable absolute being beyond qualities – consciousness itself. When Isaiah had his vision of God in the Temple, he cried in anguish that he was lost because he had gazed upon the Lord of Hosts with his own impure eyes – such an awesome sight that even the angels shielded themselves with their wings.

The prophet Ezekiel's shattering vision left him unconscious. He saw God mounted on a throne, seated on a chariot with wheels ablaze with a multitude of eyes, which was being pulled by four holy animals. The whole thing shone like brass bathed in fire. Every detail of this astounding vision was interpreted by later Jewish mystics. The four animals were seen as representing the four elements of the physical world (earth, air, fire and water), and therefore the human body. The chariot which they pulled was interpreted as a symbol for the personality. The throne mounted on the chariot was viewed as the soul. Upon this throne sits God – the 'I am' of pure consciousness at the heart of every being.

77

DESERT MYSTICS

By the time of Jesus, there were monastic groups of Jewish mystics called the Essenes living in communities in the Egyptian and Palestinian deserts. The contemporary Jewish historian Josephus, however, describes these groups as Orphics. Orphics were followers of the ancient Greek Mystery Schools of Orpheus. That the Essenes could be seen as Orphics suggests that Jewish mysticism and the Greek Mystery School tradition were practically indistinguishable. This is not surprising, since the Essenes would have undoubtedly been influenced by the Orphic and Pythagorean communities who had been living in the same desert area for centuries. There were also Buddhist ashrams which had developed from the work of missionaries sent in the third century BC by Asoka, the Emperor of India.

All these communities had much in common, living a withdrawn monastic existence away from the hustle and bustle of the world. They all believed in reincarnation and were vegetarians. All property was shared. They had two levels of initiates: only after an initial period of being a 'hearer', in which the seeker just listened, was he fully admitted into the community. The Essenes, Orphics and Pythagoreans all wore white, symbolizing purity, and practised ritual baptism.

The Jewish mystics practised a system called Hekhalot, meaning 'chambers' or 'palaces'. Using mantras, prayers, hymns, visualization and symbolic ritual, the initiate passed through a series of seven inner chambers connected by a series of bridges and guarded by angelic forces. The sage Hai Gaon explained:

> He must fast for a specific number of days, he must place his head between his knees whispering softly to himself the while certain praises of God with his face towards the ground. As a result he will gaze in the innermost recesses of his heart and it will seem as if he saw the seven halls with his own eyes, moving from hall to hall to observe that which is therein to be found.

To enter each chamber, the seeker was required to show that he possessed the necessary knowledge. Once inside, he received a spontaneous vision which revealed the secret wisdom of that particular inner state. In the seventh chamber, for example, the mystic experienced 'wonders, powers, majesty, greatness, holiness, purity, terror, humility and uprightness'. This process directly parallels Eastern yogic practices using the seven chakras; and, like their Indian counterparts, the

If any one wishes to be created afresh, then he must do everything in his power to enter the condition of nothingness, and then God will make out of him a new creation, and he will become as a spring which does not dry up and as a stream which does not cease to flow.

MARTIN BUBER
Twentieth-century
Austrian theologian

The Menorah symbolises the Angels of the Presence of God. It was taken over from the Babylonians, to whom it represented the Earth and five visible planets that surround the sun.

Jewish mystics claimed that through awakening these higher levels of consciousness psychic powers were acquired, such as the ability to foresee the future and to know a person's past lives.

The image of a seven-fold path to God is found in all mystic traditions. From Persia we read of the seven Shining Ones. The ancient Egyptians chanted seven vowel sounds to awaken divine powers. The Islamic mystics make an inner voyage through seven valleys to reach Allah. The Tibetan Buddhists journey through seven gates, each opened by a golden key. The seven sacraments in Christianity lead from baptism to the last rites. All of these traditions came originally from mystical contemplation of the seven heavenly bodies – the sun, moon and five visible planets. We still unconsciously use the image of Jacob's ladder (see below) when we describe supreme happiness as 'seventh heaven'.

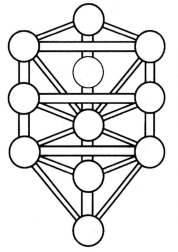

The Kaballa, or Jacob's Ladder, is the central motif of mystical Judaism. It is a map of the universe and of the human soul.

MYSTICAL KABBALA

After the destruction of Jerusalem in the first century AD by the Romans, Jewish culture was dispersed throughout the ancient world. In the thirteenth century its mystic tradition reached a great flowering in Provence in Southern France. This was the product of a meeting with two other great mystical traditions – the Cathars, a heretical group of Gnostic Christians, and the Islamic Sufi mystics who had travelled west with the expansion of the Moorish empire into Spain. All three traditions were in turn influenced by ancient Mystery School mysticism, particularly through the works of the philosopher Plotinus which were in circulation at the time and mistakenly known as 'The Theology of Aristotle'. From this interpenetration of Western spiritual traditions grew the complex mystical system of Jewish Kabbala.

'Kabbala' simply means 'tradition', and at its heart is a symbolic diagram called the Tree of Life. This is Jacob's ladder, which the mystic must climb to reach God. It is made up of ten numbered spheres. As the mystic climbs the ladder of mystical experience he is counting down – getting closer and closer to oneness. The bottom seven spheres are the seven chambers explored by the early Hekhalot pioneers. The mystic must pass safely through each one until he reaches the mysterious state of Daat, which means 'knowledge'.

Starting from Malkut, the bottom sphere, which symbolizes his body self, he ascends to Yesod, the second sphere on the middle pillar, which represents his personality. When he reaches Tiferet, the third level of the middle pillar, he finds his soul. Finally he encounters Daat, which is called the abyss. It is not one of the ten spheres, but an emptiness. From here the mystic literally takes a leap into the void, for Daat is the mystic 'knowledge' that there is no separate self. Beyond lies Keter, where God is given the name 'Ehyeh' – 'I am'. This is impersonal pure consciousness with no attributes, in which there is no longer the duality of knower or known – there is no separateness at all.

THE PATH OF NAMES

The thirteenth-century Spanish Jew Abraham Abulafia was a Kabbalist who developed a Jewish form of yoga, using the familiar methods of concentration on breathing, the repeating of mantras, and the adoption of specific physical postures to achieve heightened states of consciousness. Abulafia was a highly educated man with a deep knowledge of the Jewish scriptures, who became a mystic after an overwhelming mystical experience at the age of thirty-one. Although often outspoken in his criticisms of Christianity, he also appreciated the similarities between the essential truths of the Christian and Jewish religions. He was more concerned with direct experience than with theological theories. Some of his followers regarded him as the Messiah. Others felt that the mystical path he taught revealed to them their higher Self, which was their own Messiah and spiritual guide.

Abulafia taught that to find God it was necessary 'to unseal the soul, to untie the knots which bind it'. The soul is bound by all our ideas based on our sense perceptions, rather than our intuitive understanding. To overcome this he developed a form of meditation called the Path of Names. In deep and ecstatic contemplation, he combined and recombined the sacred letters of the Hebrew alphabet to produce different names for God. Like Hindus and Buddhists using mantras, he believed that whoever succeeded in losing himself in the names of God would attain to mystical revelations. Abulafia describes his meditative experience as like listening to musical harmonies, with the letters of the alphabet taking the place of musical notes. Another of his extraordinary experiences was of a mysterious light. He wrote:

Man is made in the image of God says the Old Testament. The four syllables of the Jewish name of God (JHVH or Jehovah/Yaweh) are arranged here in the form of a man.

After two months had elapsed and my thoughts had disengaged from everything material and I had become aware of strange phenomena occurring within me, I set myself the task at night of combining letters with one another and of pondering over them in philosophical meditation. The third night, after midnight, I nodded off a little, quill in hand and my paper on my knee. Then I noticed that the candle was about to go out. I rose to put it right, but I noticed that the light continued. I was greatly astonished after close examination to see that it issued from myself. I said, 'I do not believe it.' I walked to and fro all over the house and, behold, the light is with me; I lay on a couch and covered myself up, and behold, the light is with me all the while. I said, 'This is truly a great sign and a new phenomenon I have witnessed.'

Kabbalists often experienced extreme forms of ecstasy. Abulafia warned: 'Your whole body will be seized by an extremely strong trembling, so you will think that surely you are about to die, because your Soul, overjoyed with its knowledge, will leave your body.'

One of his followers, called Rabbi Ben Azzai, did indeed die, and another, Rabbi Ben Zoma, went mad. This is why the Kabbalists insisted that for their own safety a seeker should be guided by an experienced master, and refused to instruct anyone until he was fully mature and married. Some Jewish mystics, however, actively sought to reach such heights of ecstasy that they physically died – an experience known to the Kabbalists as 'the death of the kiss'.

THE HASIDS – GOD'S HOLY DANCERS

Eighteenth-century Poland saw the explosion of a less intellectual and totally celebratory Jewish mysticism. The Hasids or 'Devotees' were extraordinary mystics who congregated around a master called a Zaddik, which means 'Righteous One'. Their founder was the Rabbi Israel ben Eliezer, known by the title of Baal Shem, meaning 'The Master of the Holy Name'. As a young boy Baal Shem studied the Jewish scripture of the Torah in secret, and in later life would often seek the solitude of mountaintops to pray in rapture and ecstasy. He was regarded as a heretic by the orthodox rabbis because he taught that 'deliverance' lay in single-minded devotion rather than in learning the minutiae of the Jewish Holy Law.

The Hasids, although in many ways followers of tradition, were great individualists who sought their own unique relationship with God. The seventeenth-century Rabbi Nachman of Wroclaw wrote:

Every one should know and remember that his state is unique in the world, and that no one ever lived who is exactly the same as he, for had there ever been any one the same as he, there would have been no need for him to have existed. But in reality each person is a new thing in the world, and he should make his individuality complete, for the coming of the Messiah is delayed through it not being complete.

There is a Hasidic story that when a great Zaddik was criticized for not following the example of his master, he replied, 'On the contrary, I do follow his example. I leave him, as he left his teacher.'

Hasidism is a joyful mystical path, a path of the heart, whose outward expression took the form of singing and dancing. Baal Shem once took a respected book called *The Tree of Life* by the sixteenth-century Kabbalist Isaac Luria and placed it unread on the altar in the synagogue; he said that, although he did not understand it, he was sure it was full of the most sublime wisdom, and proceeded to dance around it in ecstasy. The Maggid of Mezeritch, another famous Hasidic master, once visited Baal Shem, who gave him the Kabbalist scripture of the Zohar or 'The Book of Splendour' and showed him

THE HASIDIC JEWS AND THE WAILING WALL

Although Hasidism began as a vibrant mystical form of Judaism, today it has fossilized and become ultra-conservative. Like the Christian Amish of America, who maintain the simple dress and lifestyle of the early settlers, many Hasidic Jews dress today in the same style as their predecessors in seventeenth-century Poland. Since many of them now live in the much hotter climate of Israel, their black coats and hats can seem incongruous. They maintain a strict commitment to Jewish law, including wearing an earlock of hair. They are often to be seen at prayer, rocking to and fro, by the Wailing Wall in Jerusalem. This is what remains of the second Temple destroyed by the Romans with the aim of preventing the Jews having a spiritual centre of pilgrimage to act as a unifying force within Judaism. A mosque has since been erected on the Temple Mount, which still prevents the Jews worshipping at this holy site.

how to read the holy words with all his soul. The room became full of light and the Maggid felt as though he were on Mount Sinai like Moses receiving the word of God; he became Baal Shem's disciple and later his successor.

A tale is told of a student of the Maggid of Mezeritch, who said, 'I did not go to the Maggid to learn Torah from him, but to watch him tie his boot-laces.' Like the great Hindu gurus, the Hasidic sages were living masters that the devout could learn from just being in their presence. Simply by observing the extraordinary way they lived in the world, the seeker could begin to understand the mysteries of life. The Kabbalist Isaac of Acre relates:

I have heard tell of a Hasid in Germany who was not a scholar but a simple and honest man, that he once washed away the ink from a strip of parchment on which were written prayers which included the name of God. When he learned that he had sinned against the honour of God's name, what did he do? Every day during the hour of prayer, when the congregation entered and left the synagogue, he lay down on the doorstep while old and young passed over him; and if one trod on him, whether deliberately or by accident, he rejoiced and thanked God.

Hasidism is a path of humility. Its name is sometimes interpreted as meaning 'one who bears shame'. It is a path of peaceful equanimity in the face of life's changing fortunes. Rabbi Abner tells how a 'lover of

God never does the same thing twice.

RABBI NACHMAN
Seventeenth-century Silesian Hasidic mystic

secret lore' came to a Hasidic master to be admitted as a pupil.

The master said to him, 'My son, your purpose is admirable, but do you possess equanimity or not?'

The student replied, 'Indeed, I feel satisfaction at praise and pain at insult, but I am not revengeful and I bear no grudge.'

The master told him, 'Go back to your home, for as long as you have no equanimity and can still feel the sting of insult, you have not attained to the state where you can connect your thoughts with God.'

Above all, Hasidic mysticism is a path of selfless love. A common saying was: 'What is mine is yours and what is yours is yours.' They believed that if anyone had departed from God, then the love of man was his one salvation. A father once complained to Baal Shem, 'My son has departed from God. What shall I do?' The master advised, 'Love him more.' 'Love more' was a common Hasidic maxim, and is the heart of all mysticism.

8

CHRISTIAN MYSTICISM

---◆---

Heavenly Trinity,
surpassing all essence, knowledge and goodness;
Guide of Christians to Divine Wisdom;
direct our path to the ultimate summit of Thy mystical Truth,
most incomprehensible, most luminous, and most exalted,
where the pure, absolute, and immutable mysteries
are veiled in the dazzling darkness
of the secret silence,
outshining all brilliance
with the intensity of their darkness,
and surcharging our blinded intellects
with the utterly impalpable
and invisible fairness
of glories surpassing all beauty.

ST DIONYSIUS THE AREOPAGITE
Sixth-century mystic

The empty cross, as opposed to the crucifix, is a symbol of the resurrected Jesus.

ESUS was a Jewish heretic who was put to death by the religious status quo of his day. He preached a radical mysticism that emphasized complete surrender of the self to God, through love, forgiveness and humility – a message that he embodied in his life and death. An extraordinarily influential figure whose nature is shrouded in mystery and overlaid with myth, he is pictured in many different ways by the different Christian sects which claim him as their inspiration. Like the great yogis of India, he was not confined by the 'laws' of nature that so tightly bind the rest of us. He walked on water, turned water into wine and raised the dead. For most of his followers he is an incarnation of God, comparable to the avatars of India. Whatever else Jesus may or may not have been, his wisdom shows him to have been a remarkable sage who taught with the simple authority that comes from direct knowledge of God.

From its roots in the teachings of an enlightened Jewish carpenter from Galilee, Christianity expanded via St Paul, who had previously been a persecutor of the new heretical Jewish sect but was converted by a mystical vision of divine light. By the fourth century Christianity had become the official religion of the Roman Empire, which focused on making it a dogmatic faith capable of holding the empire together rather than a personal path to knowledge of God. The Roman Church ruthlessly suppressed all the other forms of Christianity that still flourished at this time, such as the Gnostics, a highly mystical sect of mainly Jewish Christians based largely in Egypt. In this area also lived St Pachomius, who in the fourth century established the first communities of Christian monks and nuns, from which all others have developed. He was questioned by the Roman Church, which suspected him of being a Gnostic heretic, but the case was never proved.

In the fifth century the Roman Church split into a more mystical Eastern Church based in Constantinople, and an authoritarian Western Church based in Rome – both of whom proceeded to excommunicate each other. In the West, Christian mystics existed always on the edges of acceptability, often persecuted and excommunicated for their individualistic ways and heretical ideas. Despite this many great mystics still emerged, for instance the thirteenth-century Italian ascetic St Francis of Assisi. As the authoritarianism and corruption of the official Church became more and more unbearable, many groups of mystic Christians began breaking away from the suffocating power of religious dogma, to find their own direct relationship with Christ and God. A famous example is Catharism in the South of France during the twelfth century. Despite being ruthlessly suppressed, this spirit of mystical individualism persisted in heretical groups such as the Dutch and German Brothers and Sisters of the Free Spirit. It also became a powerful force in England during the turmoil of the seventeenth-century Civil War, inspiring a number of Non-Conformist sects.

The greatest flowering of Christian mysticism within the established Church was in the thirteenth and fourteenth centuries. During this time an influential anonymous mystical text called *The Cloud of Unknowing* was written in England (see p. 95), which inspired mystics such as Mother Julian of Norwich. In the Rhineland, this period also saw a number of extraordinary mystics called the Friends of God, inspired by the Dominican friar Meister Eckhart, who was excommunicated in the week he died. These mystical free thinkers influenced Martin Luther and other reformers, who eventually broke with the Roman Church. Later, however, when Protestantism itself became a religious orthodoxy, mystical ideas were once again seen as heretical and unacceptable. Protestant mystics such as the sixteenth-century German Jacob Boehme found the new religious establishment as intolerant as its precursor.

The mystics claim a direct relationship with God, which the leaders of the Christian religion have always feared as a threat to their position as the sole repositories of divine knowledge. Because of this, much of Christian mysticism has existed outside the mainstream of the Church. To find the real mystical riches of the Christian tradition

St Cuthbert sought peace on the holy island of Lindisfarne in Northern England. His miracles, however, drew a stream of pilgrims seeking healing and comfort.

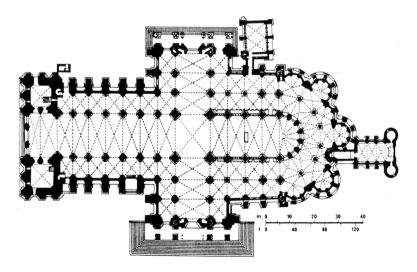

The mystical architecture of Chartres cathedral has inspired countless books dedicated to explaining its hidden meanings. Its proportions express a mystical code stretching back to ancient Egypt.

we have to look to its hidden history, which has been deliberately obscured by the establishment. Some of its greatest mystics are hardly known. Meister Eckhart, for example, an extraordinarily clear spokesman for the perennial mystic philosophy, was generally unheard of until a few decades ago. Whether they existed within the official Church or in the many heretical groups, however, the great Christian mystics have all pointed to the same essential mystic truths. Today, despite an upsurge in Christian fundamentalism, the spirit of mysticism is re-emerging. Christians such as William Johnson, Thomas Merton and Bede Griffiths have sought to incorporate elements of Eastern mysticism into the Christian faith, both to enhance their own tradition and to find a common, multicultural understanding of God.

THOMAS MERTON

The modern mystic Thomas Merton (1915–68) entered a Trappist monastery after a sudden conversion to Catholicism in 1941. He sought to isolate himself completely from society in the hope of finding God in solitude and prayer. For twenty-seven years he maintained this isolation, despite his growing fame as an author of spiritual books, and remained a strictly cloistered monk until near the end of his life. Merton taught that the ultimate truth was the realization of God through deep contemplation, and wrote: 'I have only one desire, to disappear into God, to be submerged in his peace.' He valued non-activity for its power to break through the barriers of over-organized rituals into a genuine spirituality. He wrote not 'in defence of doctrine', but as 'a meditation on the sacred mystery'. Under the influence of his close friend, the Buddhist scholar D. T. Suzuki, he moved away from a Catholic viewpoint and some authorities felt that he was preparing to renounce Catholicism in favour of becoming a Buddhist. He died in an accident while on a trip to Asia.

CHRISTIAN MYSTICAL WISDOM

The teaching of the Christian religion has generally been that Jesus was God made flesh, who suffered and died for the sins of the world, and that by believing in this a Christian is freed from sin and will go

The ressurected Jesus ascends to heaven surrounded by angels.

to heaven when he dies. Up until the Reformation in the sixteenth century, ordinary Christians were expected to accept such dogmas and the Inquisition even forbade them to read the Bible for themselves. For the mystics, however, Jesus's message was one of personal salvation through the direct experience of God. In the words of Angelus Silesius, a seventeenth-century Protestant poet who in four days of ecstatic illumination wrote the 302 verses of the mystic masterpiece *The Cherubinic Wanderer*:

> *Christ could be born a thousand times in Galilee –*
> *but all in vain, until he is born in me.*

For the mystics, Jesus was a living embodiment of the possibility of union with God, who could lead them to the same spiritual realization. In the Gnostic scripture called the Gospel of Thomas, Jesus tells his disciples: 'I am not your master. Because you have drunk, you have become drunk from the bubbling stream which I have measured out. He who will drink from my mouth will become as I am; I myself shall

This emblem of the first Christian emperor Constantine was originally a pagan symbol of life in death. It became a symbol for Christ in the 4th century.

become he, and the things that are hidden will be revealed to him.'

In the wonder of mystical experiences, when the hidden truth is revealed, the mystic knows that he is not just a body and personality that will live and then die. He is one with Christ and with God. Marsilio Ficino, a fifteenth-century Catholic priest who translated many of the great pagan philosophers for the first time and was thus instrumental in initiating the Renaissance, wrote: 'Revere yourself as an eternal ray of the Divine Sun.' Jan Ruysbroek, one of the four-teenth-century Friends of God, wrote: 'The image of God is found essentially and personally in all mankind. Each possesses it whole, entire and undivided, and all together not more than one alone. In this way we are all one.' Perhaps this is what Jesus meant when he urged, 'Love others as your self.' Not that we should love our neigh-bours to the same degree that we love ourselves, but rather that we should love others as a part of our own identity – for in truth we are all one.

To experience the oneness of God the mystic must, as the thir-teenth-century German Christian seer and poetess Mechtild of Magdeburg wrote, 'Love the nothing and flee the self.' The mystic empties himself of his sense of self, and so becomes the nothing that can contain everything. As long as he experiences himself as a 'some-thing', God is always 'other'. When he finally relinquishes the illusion of his self, there can be no 'other', and he is one with God. Jacob Boehme exclaimed: 'The Soul then says *I have nothing*, for I am utterly stripped and naked; *I can do nothing*, for I have no manner of power, but am as water poured out; *I am nothing*, for all that I am is no more than an image of Being, and only God is my I AM.'

Boehme experienced mystic union as being 'caught up in Love, as a bridegroom embraces his dear bride' – an experience he compares to being resurrected from the dead. He wrote: 'In this light my spirit suddenly saw through all. In every creature, even in herbs and grass, it knew God – who he is, and how he is, and what his will is.'

For the mystics, God is everything and everywhere. The thir-teenth-century Franciscan hermit Angela of Foligno recorded: 'I beheld in all things naught save the divine power, in a manner assuredly undescribable; so that through excess of marvelling the soul cried with a loud voice "This whole world is full of God!"'

The divine is revealed as far from contrary to the sensual world, but rather as its very life and colour. 'God is voluptuous and delicious,' rejoices Meister Eckhart. In the Gnostic Gospel of Thomas, a disciple asks, 'When will the kingdom of heaven come?'

'Not by waiting for it,' replies Jesus. 'For heaven is laid out upon the earth and men do not see it.'

We behold what we are, and we are what we behold.

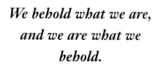

JAN RUYSBROEK

MONASTIC MYSTICISM

Christian mystics have often been hermits living a simple, reclusive life of prayer – a method of focusing the mind on God. In its highest stages prayer is silent meditation and communion with the divine. St Pachomius, who gathered together solitary hermits living in the Egyptian desert to form the first Christian monastery, experienced during prayer the mystical vision of seeing the invisible God as in a mirror. He used a still undeciphered mystical alphabet to communicate with angels.

Following the example of Jesus, who was a penniless itinerant teacher, Christian mystics have sought to transcend the personal self through a devout humility. Mechtild of Magdeburg wrote: 'The truly wise person kneels at the feet of all creatures and is not afraid to endure the mockery of others.' Monks and nuns were often encouraged to avoid using words like 'me' and 'mine', and in this way attempted to break the mental habit of seeing the world from the point of view of a separate identity. By speaking of himself not as 'I', but as 'this sinner', or 'this unprofitable servant', the mystic loosened the bonds which tied him to his ego and allowed an awareness of himself as a part of God, intrinsically and organically connected to all of life.

By humbling the self, the mystic honours the Self, which is his link to the divine. He bows down before images of Christ. He kneels in prayer and contemplation. He understands all, by standing under all. The twentieth-century Christian mystic poet T. S. Eliot writes:

> The only wisdom we can hope to acquire
> Is the wisdom of humility: humility is endless.

Why is this the only wisdom? Because spiritual knowledge is available to the mystic in proportion to his freedom from self-importance and limited personal preoccupations, which bind him to his separate self. Why is humility endless? Because compared to the vast expanses of the soul, the personality is infinitely small. As the mystic's spiritual awareness opens out, so his personal self quite naturally seems of less and less concern. He is humble in an attempt not to put himself down, but rather to lift himself up.

St Francis, the inspiration of the order of Franciscan friars, is a famous example of this spirit of humility. He was born to a wealthy family, but was disinherited by his earthly father because of his eccentric devotion to God, his heavenly father. Choosing to 'wed himself to

St Simeon spent the last 20 years of his life atop a sixty foot pillar in Syria. The deserts of Syria and Egypt in the first few centuries of the Christian era were home to thousands of Christian hermits, many of whom, like St Simeon, practised extreme austerities.

The inward man is not at all in time or place, but is purely and simply in eternity.

MEISTER ECKHART

St Thomas Aquinas

Thomas was born in 1225 in Italy, the son of a nobleman called Landulf of Aquino. He was educated by Benedictine monks in Naples, and in 1244 joined their order. Shocked at the news, his family imprisoned him in a tower for a year. However, this did not lessen Thomas's resolve to become a mendicant friar, and his family finally released him. He went to study in Paris and Cologne with St Albert the Great, a remarkable man steeped in mystical alchemy. Thomas devoted his life to writing and teaching. He constantly used the words of the Psalmist: 'Oh taste and see that the Lord is good.' He talks of mysticism as the knowledge of God through direct experience, writing: 'Great is the blindness and exceeding the folly of many souls that are ever seeking God, continually sighing after God, and frequently desiring God; whilst all the time, they are themselves the tabernacles of the living God since their soul is the seat of God in which he continually reposes.'

God is in heaven, and Heaven is in man.

Jacob Boehme

Lady Poverty', he became a travelling preacher. He saw God all around him and had a deep affinity with nature, calling the sun and moon and the elements his brothers and sisters. St Francis was a charismatic individualist, loved for his simplicity. In 1224, while praying, bleeding scars appeared on his body corresponding to the five wounds of Jesus on the Cross. These miraculous stigmata, as the phenomenon is called, never left him, causing him great pain until he finally met 'Sister Death' in 1226.

Mother Julian of Norwich is another great example of Christian humility. She was a fourteenth-century recluse who lived her life cut off from the world, permanently walled into a few small rooms attached to a church, which she never left. Nevertheless, when overcome by divine love she enthused: 'The fullness of joy is to behold God in everything.' Such recluses were called anchorites. They were interred in their permanent dwellings during a Mass for the Dead, walking into their cells as if into the grave while the presiding bishop sprinkled ashes in their wake. Such mystics symbolized in this way their dying to self and rebirth in spirit. Julian experienced an intimate relationship with God, whom she sometimes called 'Mother' and 'Husband'. She wrote: 'I saw that he is everything that is good and supports us. He clothes us in his love, envelops us and embraces us. He wraps us in his tender love and he will never abandon us.'

PAGAN CHRISTIANITY

Christianity inherited the Jewish picture of a father-God with a particular personality, who revealed himself only through certain prophets and in particular sacred scriptures. The great Christian mystics, however, sought a direct experience of the supreme impersonal oneness underlying all of life. For inspiration they turned to what may seem a surprising source – the ancient pagan mysticism of the Mystery Schools. This is not so extraordinary, however, considering that the Church Fathers St Clement and Origen of Alexandria, Gregory of Nyssa and St Augustine of Hippo, were all educated in Greek philosophy and that some of them were initiated into the ancient Mysteries. Through their influence, ancient pagan mysticism became the foundation of mystical Christianity.

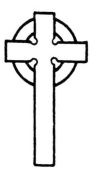

Celtic Christianity is symbolised by its distinctive cross found throughout the British Isles. Celtic Christianity was supressed by Roman Christianity in the sixth century AD.

Particularly influential was the third-century pagan initiate Plotinus. He taught that through an intuitive apprehension a mystic may experience the oneness of God, but that such a state is not found through intellectual understanding; it arises spontaneously in a mind that is silent. In his youth, St Augustine of Hippo spent four years studying Plotinus. He wrote: 'That which is called the Christian religion existed amongst the ancients and never did not exist, from the beginning of the human race until Christ came in the flesh, at which time the true religion which already existed began to be called Christianity.' As a student of Plotinus's philosophy, St Augustine had many mystical experiences. He wrote: 'In a flash of mental energy I attained to the wisdom which abides beyond all things.' He described one of his experiences in terms that could be those of a Zen Buddhist: 'My mind withdrew its thoughts from experience, extracting itself from the contradictory throng of sensuous images. And thus with the rush of one hurried glance, it attained to the vision of *That Which Is*.'

THE DAZZLING DARKNESS

Another important source of pagan influence on Christian mysticism were the writings attributed to St Dionysius the Areopagite, a contemporary of St Paul. The author was actually a sixth-century Syrian monk whose real name remains a mystery; for this reason he is often known as 'Pseudo-Dionysius'. Because he was believed to be an authoritative New Testament figure, however, his works were treated by Christian mystics with the same veneration as the biblical writings.

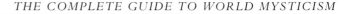
> *The Universe is in each person in such a way that each person is in it; and so every person in the Universe is the Universe.*
>
> CARDINAL NICHOLAS OF CUSA

Dionysius's writings are a subtle marriage of Mystery School mysticism and Christianity. Through him, ancient wisdom that was in danger of being lost through persecution by the official Church was smuggled into Christianity in a way that was palatable and which would have a profound and enduring influence.

Dionysius describes God as the 'Dazzling Darkness' – a beautifully evocative and paradoxical image which is remarkably similar to the Tibetan Buddhists' 'Clear Light of the Void'. God is 'darkness' because he cannot be known through thoughts, but only through ignorance – by emptying the mind of all thoughts. Dionysius teaches that God is revealed by clearing away all that he is not, 'like men who, carving a statue out of marble, remove all the impediments that hinder the clear perception of the latent image and by this mere removal display the hidden statue itself in its hidden beauty'.

Ultimately what needs to be cleared away to reveal God's 'hidden beauty' is the mystic's own opinions about God. Dionysius wrote:

> *Leave behind the senses and the operations of the intellect, that you may arise, through 'unknowing', towards the union with Him who transcends all being and all knowledge. For by the unceasing and absolute renunciation of your self and of all things, you will be borne high, through pure and entire self-abnegation, into the super essential Radiance of the Divine Darkness.*

EASTERN CHRISTIAN MYSTICISM

Whilst the theologians of the Roman Church tried hard to define God and create a creed that everyone could be forced to assent to, in the Eastern Church, centred on Constantinople, a more mystical Christianity flourished. Eastern Christians based in the Near East, on Mount Athos in Greece, and elsewhere in the Balkans were greatly influenced by Dionysius. Like him, they taught that God lay beyond the realm of thought. The fourth-century sage Gregory of Nyssa said: 'Every concept grasped by the mind becomes an obstacle in the quest to those who search.'

The fourth-century mystic Evagrius Pontus taught his monks to put aside all images and ideas, and 'approach the Immaterial in an immaterial manner'. 'Prayer means the shedding of thought,' he explains. These mystics practised a form of Christian 'yoga'.

Didochus, the fifth-century bishop of Photice, for example, taught a method in which the mystic would continually pray 'Jesus Christ, Son of God' on inhaling, and 'Have mercy upon me, a sinner' whilst exhaling – a practice which works in exactly the same way as a mantra.

For these mystics, God was known through his *energiai* – his 'energies'. In the Old Testament this energy is called God's glory. It shines out of Jesus on Mount Tabor when he is transfigured by divine rays. God makes himself known through the ceaseless activity of his energy, which the mystic too can experience as a transforming power and so become like God. In the Eastern Church, Christ crucified was not the dominant image, as it was in the West. For these mystics, the motif of Jesus shining with divine light was more important, and such a transformation was the goal of their spiritual journey.

Didochus did not believe that mystics should wait for heaven after death, as the Roman Church was teaching, but insisted that mystics could experience union with God right here and now. Whereas Western theologians thought that it was heretical for all but Jesus to declare oneness with the divine, Eastern Christian sages such as Maximus the Confessor taught: 'The whole man should become wholly God.'

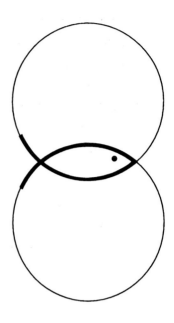

The Vessica Piscis *is derived from sacred geometry. The intersection of spirit and matter produces their 'son', the fish symbol that is still used as a sign of Jesus to this day.*

THE CLOUD OF UNKNOWING

In the medieval West, an anonymous author who translated the works of Dionysius into English for the first time also wrote a beautiful manuscript intriguingly titled *The Cloud of Unknowing*. It teaches that God is known by stilling the mind and opening the heart. He cannot be defined with the intellect, but only embraced with love. The author wrote:

> *God is always quite unable to be comprehended by the faculty of intelligence, but he is totally and perfectly intelligible by the power of love. Every single creature, moreover, will know him differently. Dwell on this if you have the grace to do so, because to experience this for oneself is everlasting joy, and the contrary is everlasting pain.*

Even in the depths of prayer and loving mediation, however, there will still remain one barrier between the seeker and God, which the author describes as 'a naked apprehension of your essential being'. To discover the all-embracing oneness of God, the mystic must relinquish his sense of self. The release from self is not within his power,

The nave of Chartres cathedral houses this labyrinth of more than twenty metres in diameter. It was walked by medieval pilgrims as a symbolic journey to the Holy Land.

but may only happen by God's grace. This could not be otherwise. If the mystic could transcend his self by his own volition, it would be like 'pulling himself up by his own bootstraps'. The one thing he definitely cannot *do* is transcend himself, for then he would remain the *doer* and so there would still be a self. The text teaches:

> *Now you are going to ask me how you can destroy this stark awareness of your self. You might be thinking that if you destroy this sense of your self you will destroy everything else too and you will be right. But I will answer this fear by telling you that without a very special grace from God and without a particular aptitude on your part, you will never be able to get rid of this naked sense of self. For your part, this aptitude consists in a robust and profound sorrow of spirit. . . . Everybody has a special reason for grief, but the person who has a deep experience of himself existing apart from God feels the most acute sorrow. Once we have acquired this sorrow it not only purifies our souls, but it takes away all the pain merited by sin and thus makes the soul capable of receiving that joy which takes from a man all sense of his own being. If this sorrow is genuine, it is full of holy longing. Otherwise nobody could bear it.*

The mystical transcendence of self is a spontaneous and natural occurrence. The author calls it 'an impromptu and unpremeditated impulse, which leaps up to God as a spark springs from the coal'. In one leap the mystic sees, but he 'quickly falls prey after each impulse to some thought or memory of some deed that he has either done or left undone'. This is part of an organic developing process, not spiritual failure by the mystic. The author optimistically writes, 'But so what? The soul can immediately spring up again as unexpectedly as it did before.'

HERETICAL CHRISTIAN MYSTICS

This 14th century fresco was found in Istanbul. The Byzantine icon of 'Christ Pantocrator', the creator of the world, has remained almost unchanged for a thousand years.

Mysticism also flourished in heretical groups outside of the established churches. One such influential sect, called the Cathars, became the prevailing religious faith in the South of France during the twelfth century. Cathar means 'Pure One', and the Cathars were barefoot models of virtue, giving all that they had to the poor, and translating the Bible from Latin into the vernacular for the very first time. This revolutionary move allowed ordinary people to read the scriptures for

THE BOGOMILS

The Cathars find their roots in the mysterious Bogomils, who have been called 'the greatest puritans of the Middle Ages'. They emerged in the Bulgarian empire around the turn of the first millennium. It was in the mountainous areas of this region that many Gnostics had taken refuge after the Emperor Constantine had made heresy a capital offence. Here they preserved secret apocryphal texts which dated from the early Christian era. These heretics claimed to be the true and hidden Church, whose wisdom stretched back to ancient Greece and beyond. Indeed, they were accused of performing ancient Mystery rites. During the twelfth century, Bogomil missionaries began to journey up the Danube. In 1142 a number of Bogomils were burnt for heresy in Cologne, which later became a centre for Cathars in Germany. The Cathars were often called by such names as 'Bulgares' and 'Bougres'. 'Bogomil' is Bulgarian for 'Beloved of God'. The Roman Church, however, used it as a term of abuse, which we have inherited as the word 'bugger'.

themselves and undermined the role of the priests. In labelling the corrupt Roman Church as the anti-Christ, however, the Cathars sowed the seeds of their own destruction. The infamous Inquisition was set up specifically to eradicate the Cathar heresy, which it did with awesome terror and violence. The year 1244 saw the climax of a bloody crusade in which thousands of Cathars – men, women and children – were burned alive. When the inquisitor who was oversee-ing this 'Final Solution' to the Cathar problem was told that his men could not tell who were initiates and who were not, he replied, 'Consign them all to the flames. God will know his own.'

Mystical free thinking endured, however, in vibrant and outrageous Christian groups such as the Little Brothers and Sisters of the Free Spirit, which flourished in Europe from the time of the Cathars until the seventeenth century. This movement attracted many extraordi-nary people including the visionary fifteenth-century Dutch painter Hieronymus Bosch, who painted many of his greatest works for the 'Brethren'. These mystical heretics declared: 'God is all that is. God is in every stone and in each limb of the human body as surely as in the Eucharist bread.' They believed that heaven and hell were states of the soul of this life, not punishments and rewards in some afterlife. Someone with direct knowledge of God carried his heaven within him, and was already 'resurrected' as a 'Spiritual'.

The vision of Jacob's Ladder with angels ascending and descending by William Blake. The Old Testament story of Jacob's dream was a favourite subject for both Jewish and Christian mystics.

I am as rich as God;
there is no grain of dust
that I do not have in
common with him.

ANGELUS SILESIUS

Novices of the Free Spirit practised various spiritual activities from self-denial, even self-torture, to the cultivation of meditative states of total passivity and serene acceptance. At some point during many years of training, mystical revelations would spontaneously occur. In the poetic words of a member of the House of Voluntary Poverty in Cologne, the practitioner would be 'wholly liquefied in Eternity'. One Sister enthused during such a revelation: 'The Soul is so vast that all the saints and angels cannot fill it. So beautiful that the beauty of the saints and angels cannot approach it. It fills all things.' Sister Catherine, author of a great heretical tract, described a series of ecstasies during which her soul 'soared up', only to descend again into her limited personal consciousness. Finally she went into a deep trance from which she declared, 'I am made eternal in blessedness. Christ has made me his equal and I can never lose that condition.' Another anonymous Free Spirit wrote: 'The Spirit of Freedom is attained when one is wholly transformed into God. This union is so complete that neither the Virgin Mary nor the angels are able to distinguish between man and God. In it one is restored to one's original state, before one flowed out of Deity.'

The orthodox Abbot of St Victor's acknowledged that these free-spirited heretics seemed outwardly pious and godly, but was still vitriolic in his condemnation of their ideas. He wrote: 'With most dangerous deceit they strive to persuade people that sinners shall not be punished, saying that sin is nothing. But the supreme madness and the most impudent falsehood is that such men should not fear nor blush to say that they are God.' The truth, however, was 'worse' than the Abbot feared! Like many mystics from all traditions, these Free Spirits claimed to have attained a oneness beyond even the idea of 'God'. The heretics of Swabia in south-west Germany claimed to mount to the pinnacle of divinity where they 'no longer had any need of God'. One woman at Schweidnitz went so far as to declare: 'When God created all things, I created all things with him. I am more than God.'

These mystical heretics believed that the only sin was to be ignorant of one's divinity, and the punishment for this was to be already in hell. One anonymous Free Spirit declared: 'Nothing is sin, except what is thought of as sin.' Another announced: 'I belong to the Liberty of Nature, and all that my nature desires I satisfy. I am a Natural Man.' They held that someone with knowledge of his divinity need only follow his spontaneous inner promptings to act well. Spiritual freedom, not moral servitude, was the will of God. Sexuality in particular became for the Free in Spirit a sacramental act. One group called the sexual act 'The delight of Paradise'. They often prac-

THE QUAKERS

Founded by George Fox, the Quakers were persecuted for their non-conformist beliefs which included pacifism, non-violence and a radical egalitarianism. Between 1661 and 1668 about twelve thousand Friends, as they called themselves, were imprisoned; more than three hundred died after cruel treatment. Besides this, many were transported overseas or had their property taken from them.

Others set sail for America of their own volition to find a safe place to practise their free spirituality in the New World. As soon as the Friends were released from jail they returned to their meeting houses and, finding them locked, practised their devotions on the streets outside. The

Quakers worshipped without any religious paraphernalia: Fox had abolished all clergy and ritual, stressing that everyone had direct personal access to God. Should their meeting be disturbed by the authorities, they would just continue in devout silence. If the members were thrown out by those attempting to break up the meeting, they would slip back in through a window and resume their quiet meditations.

Today, Quaker meetings are still silent and simple. Friends sit in contemplation. If anyone is moved by the spirit to say anything, he or she may rise and speak. When finished, the meeting returns once more to serene stillness.

tised ritual nakedness, regarding themselves as restored to the state of primal innocence that existed before the fall from the Garden of Eden. To be naked and unashamed was to be like Adam and Eve. The Free in Spirit believed that all acts were acts of God; spiritual ignorance was to believe that one's actions were one's own.

Suso of Cologne, one of the Friends of God who was heavily influenced by the Free Spirit movement, reports an extraordinary mystical experience. One bright Sunday he was sitting lost in meditation when a spiritual 'image' appeared to him and the following conversation took place:

SUSO   'Where have you come from?'
ANSWER   'I come from nowhere.'
SUSO   'What do you wish?'
ANSWER   'I do not wish.'
SUSO   'This is a miracle. Tell me what is your name?'
ANSWER   'I am called "Nameless Wildness".'

SUSO	*'Where does your insight lead?'*
ANSWER	*'Into untrammelled freedom.'*
SUSO	*'Tell me what is untrammelled freedom?'*
ANSWER	*'When a man lives by all his inclinations without distinguishing between God and himself, and without looking before or after.'*

This sense of spiritual freedom exploded in England during the mid-seventeenth-century Civil War, giving birth to a plethora of Non-Conformist groups such as the Quakers and the Ranters. The early Quakers were so named because they would 'quake' under the impact of mystical experiences. The initiator of the movement, George Fox, taught that God was to be found in silence. He abolished all clergy and ritual, stressing that everyone had direct personal access to God. Fox preached pacifism, non-violence and a radical egalitarianism. Under the pressure of persecution, members of many such groups set sail for America to find a safe place to practise their free spirituality in the New World.

THE GNOSTICS

In recent years it has become obvious that the mysticism of heretical sects such as the Cathars and the Little Brothers and Sisters of the Free Spirit actually has its roots in a form of early Christianity that was persecuted to near extinction and deliberately misrepresented by the Roman Church. Our understanding of these forgotten Christians has been revolutionized in recent years by an extraordinary archaeological discovery.

Over 1600 years ago an unknown monk hid a collection of ancient scriptures in an earthenware pot and deposited them safely inside a cave near the town of Nag Hammadi in Egypt. These texts were the heretical gospels belonging to various first and second century Christians known as Gnostics. At this time, Christianity had begun to assert itself as a hierarchical religion and to oppress all those who did not conform. These mystical texts were anathema to the Church. They were excluded from the New Testament when it was compiled as the definitive statement of Christ's life and teachings, some four centuries after his death. The owners of these extraordinary scriptures concealed them to avoid their destruction at the hands of the Church. In December 1945 a peasant named Muhammad Ali al-Samman was digging around a massive boulder when he discovered a red pot about a metre high. He relates:

It seems to me that the only true Christians were the Gnostics, who believe in self knowledge, becoming Christ themselves.

JOHN LENNON

After I broke the pot, I found a story book. I decided to bring my friends to tell them about the story. We realised immediately that this has something to do with the Christian people. And we said, 'We don't really need it at all' – it was just useless to us. So I took it to the ministry over here and he told me, 'Well, we don't really need it.' It was just rubbish for us. So I took it back home. Some of them were burned and I tried to sell some of them.

At first he had been too scared to open the jar in case it contained an evil genie. It did not. It contained the Gnostic Gospels. Despite some of these manuscripts being burned to kindle Muhammad's mother's fire, enough were preserved to transform our understanding of early Christianity. Up until their discovery, nearly all that was known of the Gnostics was written by their critics. These manuscripts, however, contain secret gospels, poems, philosophy, myths of the origins of the universe and instruction on mystical practice. They reveal an early Christianity that has a lot in common with the contemporary pagan Mystery Schools.

Tiny semi-precious gems, engraved with mystical names are some of the few items that survived the destruction of the early gnostics.

A CHRISTIAN MYSTERY SCHOOL

The Gnostics claimed to be the bearers of a secret mystical wisdom that Jesus had reserved for his closest initiates. The Secret Book of John, for example, promises to reveal the 'Mystery and the things hidden in silence'. There are intimations of this secret teaching also in the New Testament, in which Matthew asks Jesus why he uses parables when he speaks in public. Jesus replies: 'To you it has been given to know the *Mysteries* of the Kingdom of Heaven, but to them it has not been given.'

The second-century Clement of Alexandria says that, whilst normal Christian faith was 'suitable for people in a hurry', Gnostics were initiated into the Higher Mysteries. Established Christianity comprised only the Lower Mysteries, which Clement's pupil Origen called a 'popular irrational faith' – a 'worldly Christianity'. Gnosticism, by contrast, was a truly 'spiritual Christianity' concerned with the direct realization of eternal truths. Gnostic mystics claimed to have *gnosis*, meaning 'knowledge'. This was not intellectual learning, but intuitive insight into the nature of reality.

At a time when the official Church was forbidding the unbaptized to call God 'Father' and lay people were not even allowed to repeat the Lord's Prayer for themselves, the mystical Gnostics were practising an experiential Christianity in which they sought to become a 'Christ'. To the Gnostics the emerging hierarchical Church was an 'imitation Church' in place of the true Christian 'brotherhood'. In a text called the Apocalypse of Peter, the risen Jesus explains to a dismayed Peter that many believers 'will be misled' by a false Church, warning: 'Those who name themselves bishop and deacon, as if they had received their authority from God, are in reality waterless canals who do not understand the Mystery; although they boast that the Truth belongs to them alone.'

THE CHURCH OF EQUALS

The hierarchical organized church saw the Gnostic mystics, with their subversive openness of spirit and anti-authority stance, as a dangerous threat to its growing power. In the second century, the Church Father Tertullian attacked them vehemently, complaining:

How frivolous, how worldly, how merely human they are; without seriousness, without authority, without discipline, as fits their faith! To begin with, it is uncertain who amongst them has been baptised and who has not. They all have access equally; they listen equally, they pray equally – even Pagans, if any happen to come. They also share the kiss of peace with anyone who will storm the citadel of Truth with them. They are all arrogant. All offer you this 'Gnosis'.

Certain Gnostic groups developed the practice of drawing lots to see who would be the priest, who would offer the sacrament, who would act as bishop, who read the scriptures, and who would give spontaneous extempore spiritual teachings. The next time they met they would draw lots again, so that each person's role continually changed. The Gnostics believed that this system was no matter of random chance. Since God directed everything, the way the lots fell reflected his divine will.

Amongst the Gnostics, women were considered equal to men. Some were revered as teachers, prophets, travelling evangelists, priests and healers, and many Gnostic groups had women in important leadership roles.

Tertullian particularly objected to 'those women amongst the heretics' who held positions of authority. He angrily attacked 'that viper' – a woman who was the spiritual teacher of a Gnostic group in northern Africa. He was outraged, writing: 'These heretical women –

I was very disturbed and turned to myself. Having seen the light that embraces me and the good that is in me, I became divine.

ALLOGENES
Gnostic sage

how audacious they are! They have no modesty. They are bold enough to teach, and engage in discussion; they exorcise; they cure the sick, and it may be they even baptise!' The orthodox view, in Tertullian's words, was that 'It is not permitted for a woman to speak in church, nor is it permitted for her to teach, nor to baptise, nor to offer the Eucharist, nor for her to claim a share in any masculine function – not to mention any priestly office.' Although this was in line with the Jewish tradition from which Jesus had come, it is worth remembering that Jesus himself had violated these conventions by openly communicating with women and including them amongst his most intimate followers.

While the official Church was busy trying to formulate a fixed rigid creed for the faithful, the Gnostics were only interested in direct personal revelations of the truth. Indeed, they held that someone who just parroted what others had said did not have *gnosis* for himself. Anyone with personal *gnosis* had gone beyond the Church's teachings. Any 'tradition', including the Gnostic tradition, was irrelevant. The first-century sage Valentinus, teacher of a Gnostic School in Rome, writes that only someone who has come into direct contact with the 'Living One' is able to speak of God – not those with only second-hand knowledge.

The Gnostic initiate was expected to interpret the teachings he received in his own unique way. This was not seen as distorting the master's words, but as evidence of an individual's genuine understanding. To the chagrin of the established Church, these individualistic mystics were proud of the fact that nothing supported their teachings except their own insights and intuitions. The second-century North African Bishop Irenaeus complained: 'They all generate something new each day; for no one is considered initiated or mature among them unless he develops some enormous fictions!'

> *Light the lamp within you. Have a number of friends but not counsellors. Do not entrust yourself to anyone. Entrust yourself to God alone as Father and as friend.*
>
> **SILVANUS**
> **Gnostic sage**

GNOSTIC HERESIES

The supreme Gnostic heresy was to see Yahweh, the tribal deity of the Old Testament, as a false god – a vicious and foolish creator of an imperfect world. A Gnostic text called 'On the Origins of the World' writes of this false god hiding the real God both from others and from himself. The god of religion is not the God of the Gnostic mystics. A religion fixes God and defines his characteristics, but the real power of divinity is forever ineffable and can only be known through direct mystical experience, not creeds and dogmas. For the Gnostic mystics, all the villains of the Old Testament – Cain, Esau,

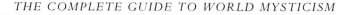

> *Seek and you will be troubled. Be troubled and you will be astonished. Be astonished and you will rule over all things.*
>
> JESUS
> **Gnostic Gospel of Thomas**

the Sodomites – become heroes for resisting the presumptuous Yahweh. A text called *The Testimony of Truth* tells the story of Genesis from the serpent's point of view. The serpent is a messenger from the true God of divine wisdom; it comes not to tempt Adam and Eve, but to guide them away from the tyrannical Yahweh and towards a direct knowledge of the true divine reality.

For the Gnostics, Jesus is not the son of a partisan Jewish god, but the son of the true God who is the oneness that underlies all. He comes not to save people from offending against the rules laid down by an autocratic creator, but directly to reveal the transcendent truth. The true God of Jesus is beyond all ideas, and so can be equally pictured as both father and mother. A Gnostic text has God declaring:

> *I am the Thought that dwells in the Light. She who exists above all. I move in every creature. I am the Invisible One within the All. I am perfection. I am knowledge. I cry out in everyone and they know a seed dwells within them. I am androgynous. I am both Mother and Father, since I make love with myself. I am the womb that gives shape to All. I am the Glorious Mother.*

The mystic Marcus, a student of Valentinus who later became a master himself, describes how divinity descended upon him in the form of a naked woman. A voice said, 'I wish to show you Truth herself; for I have brought her down from above, so that you may see her without a veil and understand her beauty.' Thus he experienced the 'naked truth' for himself.

The picture of Jesus painted by the Gnostic gospels is far from the austere 'man of sorrows' of the Church. In the Gospel of Philip it says, 'The companion of the Saviour is Mary Magdalene. Christ loved her more than the disciples and used to often kiss her on the mouth.' In the Acts of John, Jesus gathers his disciples around him in a circle and leads them in a dance in which he sings and they all answer 'amen'. He does not preach a rigid spirituality, but an intuitive mysticism. In the Gospel of Thomas, which is claimed to be written by Jesus's 'twin brother', the disciples ask Jesus, 'Do you want us to fast? How shall we pray? Shall we give alms? What diet shall we observe?' Jesus simply replies, 'Do not tell lies, and do not do what you hate.' Following this teaching, the Gnostic mystics did not obey moral codes. Rather, they believed that those with direct knowledge of God should simply follow their own inner promptings. If they wanted to be ascetics, that was God's will. If they preferred to be promiscuous, that too was God's will. The Gnostic sage Basilides even urged his followers to sin so that they would stoke the forbidden fires and reduce them to ash. The Church Father Irenaeus was not impressed, reproaching them with these words: 'They maintain that they have gone beyond all authority, and that therefore they are free to act as they please, having no one to fear. For they claim that, because they are redeemed, they cannot be judged.'

BECOMING CHRIST

The Gnostic mystics believed that Jesus had come as a spiritual guide with the power to transform his followers into his equals. In the same way that after 'enlightenment' a Buddhist becomes a Buddha, when a mystic achieved *gnosis* he was 'no longer a Christian, but a Christ'. The purpose of spiritual authority is to outgrow it. The Gospel of Philip has Jesus teaching: 'You saw the spirit, you became spirit. You saw Christ, you became Christ. You saw the Father, you shall become the Father. You see your Self, and what you see you shall become.' In the Apocalypse of Peter, the disciple relates how he was initiated by Jesus: 'The Saviour said to me, "Put your hands over your eyes and tell me what you see." But when I had done it, I saw nothing. I said, "No one see this way." He told me, "Do it again", and there came into me fear with joy, for I saw a Light, greater than the light of day.'

Simon Magus, who knew Jesus, describes each human being as a place in which 'dwells an infinite power . . . the root of the universe'. The Gnostic master Valentinus, echoing the teaching of the Mystery Schools, says that it is a person's guardian angel which conveys *gnosis* to him, but that this angelic being is actually the seeker's higher Self. He writes: 'When the human self and the divine "I" are interconnected they can achieve perfection and eternity.' The master Monoimus instructs:

> *Abandon the search for God and the creation and other similar matters. Look for Him by taking yourself as the starting point. Learn who it is within you who makes everything his own and says, 'My God, my mind, my thought, my soul, my body.' Learn the source of sorrow, joy, love, hate. . . . If you carefully investigate these matters you will find God in your Self.*

In the Dialogue of the Saviour, the disciple Matthew asks Jesus where the 'place of life, the pure light' is. Jesus replies, 'Every one of you who has known himself has seen it.' His disciples question: 'Who is the one who seeks, and who is the one who reveals?' Like a Zen master, Jesus answers that 'The one who seeks is also the one who reveals.'

When you make the two as One, and the inside like the outside, you will enter the Kingdom of Heaven.

JESUS
Gnostic Gospel of Thomas

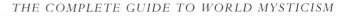

> *Do not be ignorant of me anywhere at any time.*
>
> GOD
> **Gnostic Gospels**

In the Testimony of Truth, Jesus advises a follower to become a disciple of his own mind because it is the 'Father of Truth'.

The sage Valentinus gives the central Gnostic teaching, which is the same perennial wisdom taught by all Christian mystics and, indeed, all other mystical traditions: 'Knock on yourself as upon a door and walk upon yourself as on a straight road. For if you walk on this road, it is impossible to go astray. Open the door for yourself that you may *know*.' For as Jesus himself says in the New Testament, 'The Kingdom of Heaven is within you.'

9

ISLAMIC MYSTICISM

♦

If you want to be immortal and exalted,
first get rid of your self,
then summon a winged horse out of nowhere,
to carry you away.
Clothe yourself with garments of nothingness,
and drink a cup of annihilation.
Cover your heart with nothingness,
and your head with a robe of non-existence.
Put your foot in the stirrup of renunciation,
and looking straight ahead,
ride the steed of non-being
to the palace of emptiness.
You'll get lost over and over again,
but travel with equanimity,
until at last you reach the world
where you are completely lost altogether.

ATTAR
Twelfth-century Sufi saint

The star and the crescent is the emblem of Islam. It represents the prophet Mohammad and the angel Gabriel who dictated the Koran to him.

'*ISLAM*' means 'surrender', and at its heart is the mystical teaching of surrendering to God – of abandoning the self and its personal will, and embracing the divine will. This religion of surrender was born out of the mystical revelations of its founder, the seventh-century prophet Muhammad. He was a simple man, who grew up in poverty as an orphan. As an adult he became a moderately successful businessman in the city of Mecca, but tragically most of his children died. The Arab culture in which he grew up was beginning to be heavily influenced by Jewish and Christian monotheistic ideas, and Muhammad drew on both of these traditions when he came to found Islam.

He loved the solitude of the deserts and mountains, where he would go to meditate on 'Allah', which means 'The God' (Al-Lah). He was ascending Mount Hira, as he did for a month every year to practise his devotions, when he heard the stones and trees honour him by calling him 'the Prophet of God'. Later, whilst meditating in a cave, he started receiving visits from the angel Gabriel. On one occasion he saw this angelic being as a colossal figure with one foot astride each horizon, and wherever he looked he saw this vision. During one of these mystical experiences, Gabriel pressed a written text against the prophet's forehead and commanded him to read. Muhammad was almost illiterate, so the angel impressed the words upon his heart. The revelations that he received in this way became the Qur'an – the holy scripture that is the foundation of Islam. After these revelations Muhammad wrote letters to all the world leaders, explaining his new religion.

Muhammad is said to have made a mystical journey on a winged horse, which carried him by night to the Temple Mount in Jerusalem. Here he was greeted by Abraham, Moses, Jesus and other great prophets. Then Gabriel and Muhammad began a perilous ascent up a mystical ladder to the 'seventh heaven', a metaphor for the highest spiritual experience. The Qur'an describes Muhammad in this exalted state: 'By the lote-tree of the furthest limit, near the Garden of Promise, which the lote-tree veiled in a veil of nameless splendour . . . truly did he see some of the most profound of his Sustainer's symbols.' Interestingly, in Hinduism the lote-tree is a symbol which marks the limits of rational thought. In his vision, Muhammad sees God through his most elevated symbols. He has reached the very edges of the rational mind – the threshold of the supreme mystical experience of which nothing may be said.

The religion founded by Muhammad requires the faithful to be devout. A Muslim is expected to pray five times a day while facing towards the holy city of Mecca, to which they are also required to make a pilgrimage at least once during their lifetime, if at all possible. All work is to be performed as devotion to God, and material generosity is regarded as an essential spiritual quality. In the spring month of Ramadan, Muslims fast from dawn till dusk.

Muhammad's new religion united the many warring Arab tribes into a peaceful federation. As Islam became an established hierarchical religion, however, it became more doctrinaire and authoritarian. In reaction to this loss of mystical spirituality, heretical groups of spiritual individualists arose. They became known as Sufis.

The Sufis were the ecstatic mystics of Islam, many of whom were great poets; some, like the eleventh-century Omar Khayyám, were also eminent scientists and mathematicians. Sufism is a passionately devotional path to union with God. It began around the end of the eighth century with a group of mystics called the Baghdad School, which included Rabi'a (d. 801), a woman poet and ascetic, and Bayazid of Bastami (d. 874) who, like Rabi'a, approached God as a lover and strove to please Allah as he would a woman. By 922 the Sufis were regarded as dangerous heretics and some, like al-Hallaj, were executed by the Islamic authorities. Sufism flowered under the influence

IRINA TWEEDIE

Irina Tweedie was born in Russia in 1907. As an adult, she lived a happily married life in England until the early death of her husband. Distraught, she set off on a spiritual quest that led her to the feet of a Sufi master in India. Her teacher had little time for religion but, by being both confronting and compassionate, he led her step-by-step to an inner encounter with herself. She describes the prelude to her mystical experience of liberation as 'the slow grinding down of the personality – a painful process for man cannot remake himself without suffering. I had hoped to get instruction, but found myself forced to face the darkness within myself. I was beaten down in every sense until I had come to terms with that in me which I had been rejecting all my life.' Drawing on traditional Islamic imagery, she wrote: 'The Path of Love is like a bridge of hair across a chasm of fire.'

of the great poet-mystic Rumi (d. 1273), but by 1400 it had passed its peak and become little more than a cult of dead saints.

Today, despite the growth of Muslim fundamentalism, there is resurgence of interest in this colourful and ecstatic mystic tradition.

THE WISDOM OF THE SUFIS

In the early Middle Ages the powerful Islamic world was fighting the Crusades against the Christian infidels in the name of Allah, justifying itself by Muhammad's talk of the 'Jihad' or 'Holy War'. But the Sufis interpreted this idea as an internal battle to overcome the self and surrender to God. They believe that our normal state of awareness is a type of sleep and that, as Muhammad had said, death is a waking up. Human beings live in a sort of painful and pleasurable dream. The prophet taught, however, 'Die before you die', and the Sufis believe that it is possible to 'wake up' to reality here and now, through surrendering to God. They see themselves as making a 'migration' beyond the world, to a direct experience of Allah. This mystical journey of awakening is the very purpose of life.

In a Sufi teaching story, the Prince of Blakh was lost in a desert while hunting. The stag which was his quarry was a magical animal, however, and turned to him, asking, 'Were you really born for this?' For the Sufis, it is important to ask ourselves, 'Am I fulfilling the purpose of my life?' The great thirteenth-century mystic poet Jala ud-Din Rumi wrote:

> *There is one thing that must never be forgotten. If you were to forget everything else, but were to remember this one thing, there would be no cause for regret; while if you remembered, performed and attended to everything else, but forgot this one thing, you would in fact have done nothing whatsoever. It is as if a king had sent you to a country to carry out one special, specific task. You go to the country and you perform a hundred other tasks, but if you have not performed the task you were sent for, you have performed nothing at all. So man has come into the world for a particular task, and that is his purpose. If he doesn't perform it he will have done nothing.*

The Sufis believe we are born with the purpose of discovering our true spiritual nature. The Qur'an teaches that Allah created Adam in his image so that he could contemplate himself as if in a mirror; the Sufis therefore believe that our deepest identity is as God. The Sufi path is one of abandoning the limited personal self and in so doing becoming an empty nothingness filled with God. Muhammad Iqbal, the early twentieth-century Sufi who was also an eminent lawyer and statesman, wrote: 'Who are you looking for? What passion fills you? God is plainly visible, you are the veil.'

The Sufis tell a story of a man who knocks on a door. 'Who's there?' asks God from within.

'It's me,' says the man.

'Go away, then,' says God.

'There's no room here for "me".'

The man departs and wanders in the dry desert until he realizes his error, returns to the door and knocks again.

'Who's there?' asks God.

'Thou,' answers the man.

'Then come in,' God replies.

For the Sufis, abandoning the 'me' of the separate self is the beginning and end of the mystical journey. The fourteenth-century Sufi sage Shah Ne'matollah Wali teaches: 'Just take one step outside your self. The whole path lasts no longer than this step.'

Rumi encourages us to take this mystical step, writing in one of his poems:

> *Why are your lips dry when the cup is full?*
> *Conceive an impossible plan – as Noah did!*
> *Live the life that you love.*

The crazy project he has in mind is mystical union with God – yet the real craziness is to be full of the waters of life and not to drink. For the Sufis, God cannot be found in the rites and dogmas of religion, but only through direct mystical experience. Each individual must drink of the waters of life for himself.

> *When you seek Him, look for Him in your looking. Closer to you than yourself to yourself.*
>
> JALA UD-DIN
> RUMI

LOVERS, DRUNKS AND FOOLS

Sufis are famous for their ecstatic devotional poetry. Originally, these verses were spontaneously improvized by spiritual masters while in states of mystical rapture. To express the intensity of their passion for God, these mystic poets turned to the evocative language of romantic love. The fifteenth-century Indian Muslim poet Kabir, whose teacher was a Hindu, writes of God like one longing for his absent lover:

Heart broken in two –
I am separate
from my lover.
Days without comfort.
Nights without sleep.
Can you comprehend this longing?
Love is absent.
The dark hours wander aimlessly.
I start up –
trembling all over with fear.
Kabir says: 'Listen to me.
Only the lover can satisfy you.'

Ayn Hamadani, a Sufi saint who was executed by the Muslim author-ities for heresy in 1098, expresses his relationship with the divine in beautiful sensual imagery:

She embraced me in the night.
My idol entwined me in her arms.
She captured me and pierced me
with a ring that showed I was her slave.
I exclaimed 'For this loving I'll cry, I'll rage, I'll frenzy. . . .'
but she closed my mouth with her sweet lips.

The eleventh-century saint Ahmad Ghazali, who wrote a mystic book called *The Secrets of Unity*, was the first to use the important Sufi image of the seeker being drawn to the love of God like a moth attracted to the light of a candle, until it flies so close that its wings are singed and it dies into the light. In the same way, by abandoning his self in ecsta-tic love the Sufi mystic dies into union with God.

Although alcohol is forbidden to Muslims, the Sufi poets often use the imagery of inebriation to describe the joy of their mystical elation. Gharib Nawaz, a twelfth-century saint whose shrine is known as the Mecca of India, exclaims in God-intoxicated ecstasy: 'Every atom in me longed for a vision, until I collapsed drunk on your manifesta-tions.' The thirteenth-century Sufi poet Forughi Bastami begs:

Drown me in an ocean of wine,
before my small boat is pulled down
by the whirlpool of time!

The Sufi saints are also renowned for their 'foolish wisdom'. Like the eccentric Hindu gurus, they often act in bizarre and seemingly sense-less ways to guide those around them on the mystic path. Sufis tell teaching stories about a character called Mullah Nasrudin, who

Non-existence within existence is my rule. Getting lost in getting lost is my religion.

AYN HAMADANI
Twelfth-century
Sufi mystic

teaches through his craziness. In one story Nasrudin brings a gift to a powerful Sultan. 'I have brought you a picture of the biggest fool in your realm,' he tells the powerful leader.

The Sultan is delighted and unwraps his gift. His pleasure turns to fury, however, when he finds he is looking into a mirror. 'Take this impudent man away and have him flogged,' he commands.

Nasrudin is astonished and looks in the mirror to see what has caused offence. 'But your majesty,' he protests, 'this *is* a picture of the greatest fool in your realm.'

MAGICAL POWERS

Sufi groups revolve around great teachers called Shaikhs, who often possess miraculous powers. They practise secret methods to achieve union with God through trance, meditation, breathing techniques, dance and song. The Whirling Dervishes were a Sufi group founded by Rumi, and induce ecstasy through swirling dances. In this practice, which developed from pre-Islamic shamanic mystic techniques, the Sufis gyrate around a central Shaikh to symbolize the movement of the planets circling the sun. The dancers are called 'Lovers of God' and the Shaikh is known as 'Doctor of the Heart', 'Spring of Knowledge', 'Exalted Rose'. Whilst reciting the name of Allah like a mantra, the Dervishes whirl both on their own axis and about the teacher. To the music of drums, flutes and strings they dance ecstatically with eyes closed, until they collapse into the sublime stillness of union with God.

The Enneagram (nine points that surround the central tenth), is a symbol of cosmic harmony. It was used by Islamic Sufis and later by Gurdjieff and his followers.

The Rifaiya or Howling Dervishes chant in a circle while violently moving their bodies. They also walk on fire, swallow red-hot coals, handle poisonous snakes, fall on knives and eat glass! Whilst such techniques are respected as a means of self-transcendence, the acquisition of magical powers for their own sake is seen as a dangerous distraction which actually inflates the seeker's ego. This teaching is brought out by a traditional Sufi tale about the great sage known as Issa Son of Miryam, which is the Sufi name for Jesus son of Mary, whom they treat as a prophet of God.

Issa was walking in the desert near Jerusalem with his followers, who begged him to tell them the secret name which gave him the power to raise the dead. He said, 'If I tell you, you won't use it wisely.' They replied, 'We are ready, master, and it will strengthen our faith.'

'You don't know what you are asking,' he told them.

They insisted, however, so he revealed the name.

A little later, these people left Issa and came upon a heap of

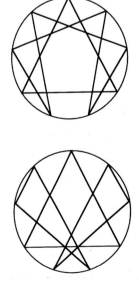

whitened bones. 'Let's try out that magic name,' one of them suggested – so they did. In an instant the bones became clothed with flesh and were transformed into a wild beast which tore them all to shreds. Such is the danger of knowledge without the wisdom to use it.

'I AM GOD!'

Jesus was important to many Sufis, particularly the great eleventh-century master al-Hallaj. Like Jesus, in the ecstasy of union with God he announced, 'I am the Truth! I am God!' And like the Jewish priests that put Jesus to death, the Islamic authorities were appalled and had al-Hallaj crucified as a heretic. As the Cross was being prepared for him, he turned to those present and said:

> *Oh Lord, forgive these your servants, who from religious zeal and the desire to win your favour have gathered here to kill me. Have mercy on them, for if you had revealed to them what you have revealed to me, they would not be doing this. And if you had hidden from me what you have hidden from them, I would not have to suffer this. Glory to you, whatever you do and whatever you will.*

When the great mystics claim to be God, it can sound grandiose and inflated. Certainly this is the case with 'false prophets' who have not transcended their egos, but simply enlarged them. A Sufi story clarifies this difference between transcendence and inflation. It concerns a dream experienced by one of the Muslims who participated in the torture and murder of al-Hallaj. The dreamer is confused to see the heretical Sufi being ceremoniously taken up to heaven. He asks, 'Oh, God! Why was a pharaoh condemned to the flames for crying out, "I am God", and al-Hallaj is swept away to heaven for crying out the same words?' Then he hears a divine voice saying, 'When pharaoh spoke these words, he thought only of himself, and had forgotten Me. When al-Hallaj uttered these words – the same words – he had forgotten himself and thought only of Me. Therefore "I am God" in pharaoh's mouth was a curse to him, but in al-Hallaj's mouth this "I am God" is the effect of My grace.'

When the personality thinks it is God, we have the egomaniac. When the personality surrenders itself to God, we have the enlightened saint. Not all self-transcendent experiences are mystical. The confused madman, like the inflated false prophet, may have lost his sense of self – however, he has exchanged it not for a sense of God, but for no sense at all. Likewise those who lose themselves in frenzied mass hysteria, like the participants and audience at the Nazis'

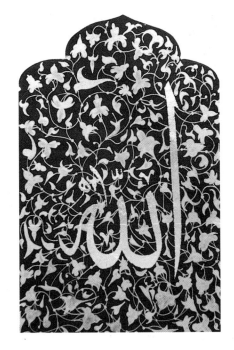

Forbidden by religious laws from making any image of man beast or God, Islamic artists turned caligraphy into high art. The name of Allah depicted here was a particularly popular subject.

Nuremberg rallies, may be said to have gone beyond their separate selves, but only by trading their little limited egos for a massive limited ego such as that of German fascism. Losing oneself in patriotic fervour or being swept along by herd instinct can feel pleasantly liberating, precisely because we are no longer caught within the confines of our personal prison cell and have become participants in a greater transpersonal identity. The end result, however, is not a lessening of the sense of 'me' and 'mine', but its strengthening. Such experiences of false transcendence are always marked by an 'us' and 'them' attitude of mind. This is not the mystic path to unity. It ultimately increases separation, bringing only suffering and confusion.

PAGAN ISLAM

At the centre of Sufi philosophy is the idea of Tawhid, which means 'Making One' – a central teaching of Islam. Like the Christian mystics, however, the Sufis also owe much to the pagan Mystery Schools, who likewise have the oneness of God at the centre of their philosophy. The originally tolerant Islamic world inherited much ancient wisdom that was exiled along with pagan sages forced to flee east through relentless persecution in the Christian West. The writings of the mystic Plotinus were of particular influence with the Sufis, as they

To undertake the 'Haj' or pilgrimage to Mecca at least once in their lives is the duty of all good Muslims. In the Islamic mystical imagination the black stone is really a white pearl.

were for the Christian mystics. Some authorities say that the name 'Sufi' comes from the word for wool, and refers to the humble clothing they typically chose to wear. Others, however, say it derives from the name of the Greek Goddess of Wisdom, Sophia.

Sophia was certainly important to many Sufis, for instance the twelfth-century saint Ibn Arabi who experienced visions from an early age. His follower Sadruddin Quyawi says of him: 'Our teacher had the power to meet the spirit of any dead prophet or saint, either by making him descend to the level of the world and contemplating him in an apparitional body similar to the sensible body of his person, or by making him appear in his dreams, or by unbinding himself from his material body to rise to meet the spirit.'

Ibn Arabi had a vision of the goddess Sophia while circling the Holy Ka'aba in Mecca. The Ka'aba is a black meteorite that fell from the heavens and was originally dedicated to the goddess, just like the black stone in the pagan shrine at Delphi. Muslims ritually circle the Ka'aba, which represents the still hub at the centre of the wheel of change. One day, while Ibn Arabi was performing such ritual circum-ambulations, a hand touched his shoulder. 'I turned round and found myself in the presence of a young girl,' he wrote, describing her as 'a priestess, a daughter of the Greeks, in whom I witnessed a radiant source of light'. The profound influence of pagan mysticism on this Sufi saint is so clear that he is still known as Ibn Aflatun – the Son of Plato.

The twelfth-century Sufi philosopher Suhrawardi made it his life's work to link Islam with what he called 'the original Oriental religion'. He taught that all the ancient sages had followed a single perennial philosophy, which was originally revealed to the great Egyptian master Hermes. Hermes was venerated as a god in the Greek Mystery Schools. In Egypt he was known as Thoth. Suhrawardi identified him with the prophet called Idris in the Qur'an and Enoch in the Apocrypha. The wisdom of Hermes, Suhrawardi taught, had been secretly handed down from sage to sage, until it had finally reached himself via al-Hallaj. This mystic philosophy could be found at the heart of all religions by those who sought it. Suhrawardi, like his master al-Hallaj, was executed for heresy by the authorities.

TOLERANCE

Despite being persecuted themselves, the Sufis were extremely tolerant of other traditions. Ibn al-Arabi taught that there was one God who inspired all religions, and he was to be found in mosque, temple, synagogue and church alike. The only mistake was to see any man-made idea of God as identical with the true transcendent divinity. He wrote: 'Do not attach yourself to any particular creed exclusively, so that you disbelieve all the rest; otherwise you will miss much that is good, indeed, you will fail to see the real Truth. God the omnipotent and omnipresent is not contained by any one creed, for He says in the Qur'an, "Wherever you turn, there is the face of Allah."'

Rumi taught that there was no universal 'right way' to approach God – each seeker must follow the dictates of his own heart. He tells an amusing tale about Moses, who one day overheard a humble shepherd talking to God. The shepherd's tone was relaxed and familiar. He told God how he wanted to help him – to pick the lice off him, to wash his clothes, to kiss his hands and feet. He ended his prayer with, 'When I think of you all I can say is "Ahhhh!".'

Moses was appalled and exclaimed, 'Do you realize you are talking to the creator of heaven and earth – not to your old uncle?'

The shepherd repented of his ignorance and wandered sadly off into the desert.

But God rebuked Moses, saying; 'What to you seems wrong is right for him. One man's poison is another man's honey. Purity and impurity, sloth and diligence – what do these matter to me? I am above all that. Ways of worship cannot be put in ranks as better and worse. It is all praise and it is all right. It is the worshipper who is glorified by worship – not I. I don't listen to the words. I look inside at the humility. Only that low and open emptiness is real. Forget language – I want burning, burning! Be friends with this fire. Burn up your ideas and your special words.'

Like the great mystics from all spiritual traditions, Sufis such as Rumi were not concerned with religious creeds and dogmas, but with finding a direct and intimate knowledge of God. This, all the mystics tell us, can only be found by looking within and finding our own deeper identity. God does not reside in sacred books or holy buildings, but in the hidden recesses of the human heart. Rumi wrote:

> *I looked for Him on the Christian cross,*
> *But he was not there.*
> *I went to Hindu temples and shrines – but nothing.*
> *I visited the Ka'aba in Mecca,*
> *I did not find Him.*
> *I questioned learned scholars,*
> *But He outstripped their understanding.*
> *Finally, when I peered into my own heart –*
> *There, and nowhere else, was His home.*

They say the path is difficult.
Allah forgive them!
I passed so easily.
The Holy Spirit is my every breath.
Perhaps I am the second Jesus – who can say?

GHARIB NAWAZ
Twelfth-century
Sufi mystic

10

MYSTICISM OUTSIDE RELIGION

◆

As I sat in the midst of the tangled metal,
I felt my individual boundaries begin to melt.
I started to merge with everything around me –
with the policemen, the wreck,
the workers with crowbars trying to liberate me,
the ambulance, the flowers on a nearby hedge,
and the television cameramen.
Somewhere, I could see and feel my injuries,
but they did not seem to have anything to do with me;
they were merely part of a rapidly expanding network
that included much more than my body.
The sunlight was unusually bright and golden
and the world seemed to shimmer with a beautiful radiance.
I felt blissful and exuberant.
The accident and the experience that accompanied it
totally transformed my world-view
and my way of understanding existence.

A car accident survivor

MYSTICAL EXPERIENCES are happening all the time, to ordinary people living ordinary lives, who are not part of any spiritual tradition and who do not necessarily consider themselves at all religious. The whole of life is a journey of awakening in which any event can suddenly trigger a spontaneous mystical revelation of a deeper reality than the one we habitually experience. That event could be a car crash, a bereavement, a love affair, foreign travel, unexpected luck or misfortune, illness, sex, war – indeed anything that frees someone for a moment from the personality he believes himself to be, and so reveals the spark of the divine which is his soul, and the ever-present power of love which permeates and sustains the universe.

In a recent Gallup Poll, one in ten Americans claimed to have had an out-of-body experience. Researchers have found that most terminally ill patients who are conscious at the time of death experience vivid visions of 'indescribable beauty'. Science has now amassed many thousands of reports of near-death experiences – stories of those who have clinically died and yet returned to tell the tale. Amongst the mystical wonders recounted, there is an almost universal experience of a transcendental being of light. One such patient recalls: 'When the light appeared, the first thing he said to me was, "What have you done with your life?" All through this, he kept stressing the importance of love . . . and knowledge too.'

Many of us have had extraordinary experiences that we overlook because we do not know what to make of them, or because they 'just happened' for no apparent reason. But the mystical experience always has this quality of an undeserved gift, of a miracle, of 'grace'. Realization cannot be forced or demanded, the mystics tell us, but arises naturally and spontaneously. It may arise after performing spiritual disciplines such as prayer and meditation, but it often visits at the most surprising of times when it is least expected. A modern woman recalls an unexpected experience as a nine-year-old girl: 'Suddenly the Thing happened, and, as everybody knows, it cannot be described in words. I remember saying to myself, in awe and rapture, "So it's like this; now I know what Heaven is like, now I know what they mean in church."' A Mr J. Trevor remembers returning from the local pub:

The sun as giver of all life is perhaps the supreme symbol of the deity.

I walked along the road to the Cat and Fiddle, and then returned. On the way back, suddenly, without warning, I felt that I was in Heaven – an inward state of peace and joy and assurance indescribably intense, accompanied with a sense of being bathed in a warm glow of light; a feeling of having passed beyond the body. These highest experiences that I have had of God's presence have all been rare and brief – flashes of consciousness which have compelled me to exclaim with surprise, 'God is here.'

Warner Allen writes in his book *The Timeless Moment* of being surprised by rapture and trying to express his insight in a jumble of incoherent sentences: 'Something has happened to me – can this be that? (*That* being the answer to the riddle of life) – but it is too simple – I always knew it – it is remembering an old forgotten secret – like coming home – I am not "I", not the "I" I thought – there is no death – peace passing all understanding.'

Many people have experienced such spontaneous mystical experiences through the beauty of nature. A nature mystic of this kind was the nineteenth-century English writer Richard Jefferies. He was regarded in his lifetime as an atheist, but the descriptions of his mystical visions contained in his autobiography *The Story of My Heart* display the same enthusiasm and insight as the great sages of the world's religions. He wrote: 'Realising that spirit, recognising my own inner consciousness, the psyche so clearly, I cannot understand time. It is entirely now. I am in the midst of it. It is all about me in the sunshine; I am it, as the butterfly floats in the light-laden air. Nothing has to come. Now is eternity; now is the immortal life. Here this moment, by this hill, on earth, now; I exist in it.'

MYSTIC POETS

Excuse my enthusiasm – or rather madness, for I am drunk with intellectual vision.

WILLIAM BLAKE
Mystic poet

Experiences of altered states of awareness have inspired many great poets, artists and musicians. They include the eighteenth-century English Romantic William Blake, whose epitaph reads 'poet and mystic'; another English Romantic William Wordsworth, who wrote of the mystic inspiration he received from communing with nature; the Irish poet W. B. Yeats, who was a member of the occult fraternity of the Golden Dawn, which was inspired by the ancient Mystery Schools; Robert Graves, who became a modern devotee of Isis, the White Goddess of the ancient Egyptians; T. S. Eliot, who recorded his mystical experiences in the sublime poems of 'The Four Quartets';

and modern blues singer-songwriter Van Morrison, who sings 'Hymns to the Silence'.

The seventeenth-century poet Thomas Traherne recorded that he was suddenly overcome by ecstatic delight while witnessing the wonders of a city street:

The dust and stones of the street were as precious gold. The gates at first were the end of the world. The green trees transported and ravished me; their sweetness and unusual beauty made my heart to leap, and almost mad with ecstasy, they were such strange and wonderful things. The men! Oh what venerable and reverend creatures did the aged seem! Boys and girls playing in the streets were moving jewels. I knew not that they were born or should die. But all things abided eternally as they were in their proper places. Eternity was manifested in the light of day, and something infinite behind everything appeared. The city seemed to stand in Eden, or to be built in heaven.

The nineteenth-century English poet Alfred, Lord Tennyson experienced from boyhood a 'waking trance', produced by the simple means of silently repeating his own name. He reported: 'Out of the intensity of consciousness of individuality, individuality itself seemed to dissolve and fade away into boundless being, and this is not a confused state but the clearest, the surest of the sure, utterly beyond words – where death was an almost laughable possibility – the loss of personality seemed no extinction, but the only true life.'

The nineteenth-century American poet Walt Whitman wrote of his mystical visions with the power of an Old Testament prophet. He is a remarkable example of a spontaneous mystic who was part of no religious tradition. From his own direct experience he discovered the perennial mystic philosophy which informs all his work. Only later in life did he draw on the inspiration of traditional spiritual philosophy like that contained in the Hindu *Upanishads*. He not only spontaneously experienced the depth of insight of the great saints, but also embodied the same spiritual qualities, and could be called a 'natural sage'. His friend Dr Bucke wrote of him:

Perhaps, indeed, no man who ever lived liked so many things and disliked so few as Walt Whitman. All natural objects seemed to have a charm for him. He appeared to like all the men, women and children he saw. I never knew him to argue or dispute, and he never spoke about money. He always justified, sometimes playfully, sometimes quite seriously, those who spoke harshly of himself or his writings. When I first knew him, I used to think that he watched himself, and would not allow

You walk, as it were, round yourself in the revelation.

XENOS CLARKE
Nineteenth-century philosopher and psychedelic mystic

his tongue to give expression to fretfulness, antipathy, complaint, and remonstrance. It did not occur to me as possible that these mental states could be absent in him. After long observation, however, I am satisfied that such absence or unconsciousness was entirely real. He never spoke deprecatingly of any nationality or class of men, or time in the world's history, or against any trades or occupations – not even against any animals, insects, or inanimate things, not any of the laws of nature, nor any of the results of those laws, such as illness, deformity, and death. He never swore. He could not very well, since he never spoke in anger and apparently never was angry. He never exhibited fear, and I do not believe he ever felt it.

PSYCHEDELIC MYSTICISM

In recent years, many people have consciously sought altered states of awareness outside the context of a spiritual tradition, through the use of psychedelic drugs. This began in the nineteenth century with the synthesizing of artificial drugs, which coincided with the birth of psychology – the scientific study of the nature of the mind. William James, who wrote a seminal study of mysticism entitled *The Varieties of Religious Experience*, was one of these Victorian pioneers of psychedelic mysticism. He experimented with ether and nitrous oxide at Harvard University, concluding that they 'stimulate the mystical consciousness in an extraordinary degree. Depth beyond depth of truth seems revealed to the inhaler.' In words reminiscent of the spiritual revelations of sages and saints from the great world religions, he wrote: 'It is as if the opposites of the world, whose contradictoriness and conflict make up all our difficulties and troubles, had melted into unity.'

One of James's fellow-experimenters likewise reported 'The *other* in its various forms appears absorbed into the One.' Benjamin Paul Blood, writing in 1874 of his experiences of anaesthetic, boldly announced: 'The Anaesthetic Revelation is the Initiation of Man into the Immortal Mystery of the Open Secret of Being.' He describes the experience of discovering his soul or 'genius' whilst in drug-induced rapture: 'Into this pervading Genius we pass forgetting and forgotten, and thenceforth each is all, in God. There is no higher, no deeper, no other, than the life in which we are founded. The One remains, the many change and pass; and each and every one of us *is* the One that remains.'

Like all ecstatic mystics, this Victorian adventurer into inner space

The sway of alcohol over mankind is unquestionably due to its power to stimulate the mystical faculties of human nature. Sobriety diminishes, discriminates and says 'no'; drunkenness expands, unites and says 'yes'.

WILLIAM JAMES
The Varieties of Religious Experience

exclaims, 'I know the meaning of Existence: the sane centre of the universe – at once the wonder and the assurance of the Soul.' Of his 'patients' who took part in his psychedelic experiments, Blood wrote:

> *No words may express the imposing certainty of the patient that he is realising the primordial, Adamic surprise of Life. Repetition of the experience is ever the same, as if it could not possibly be otherwise. The subject resumes his normal consciousness only to partially and fitfully remember its occurrence, and to try to formulate its baffling import – with only this consolatory afterthought; that he has known the oldest truth, and that he has done with human theories as to the origin, meaning, or destiny of the race. He is beyond instruction in 'spiritual things'.*

Like a shaman experiencing ritual death of his separate ego, another Victorian psychedelic pioneer, J. A. Symonds, described his revelations while under the influence of chloroform as taking him to the very threshold of his mortality where he encountered a divine being of light:

> *I seemed at first in a state of utter blankness; then came flashes of intense light, alternating with blackness. I thought I was near death; when, suddenly, my Soul became aware of God, who was manifestly dealing with me, handling me, so to speak, in an intense personal present reality. I felt him streaming in like light upon me . . . I cannot describe the ecstasy I felt.*

The use of cannabis as a stimulant of the mystical imagination is as old as human history. It is still used by some Indian holy men today as an aid in initiation rites.

ALL YOU NEED IS LOVE

The explosion of mysticism in the West during the 1960s was fuelled by the use of various hallucinogens, particularly hashish and LSD. Like William James in the nineteenth century, Dr Timothy Leary experimented with psychedelic drugs whilst teaching at Harvard University. His fellow explorer was Dr Richard Alpert, who later sought a spiritual context for his experiences by travelling in India, where he met his guru Neem Karoli Baba who gave him the name Ram Dass. Like the great mystics in previous centuries, Leary and Alpert were persecuted by the fearful authorities. They were expelled from Harvard as a result of the controversy that their work provoked, and Leary was later imprisoned. However, they initiated a cultural revolution that had at its centre the first-hand mystical encounters of millions of people.

TIMOTHY LEARY

Harvard professor Timothy Leary was one of the most charismatic spokesmen of the American counter-culture in the 1960s. His most famous slogan, which became a rallying cry for a generation, was 'Turn on, tune in, drop out.' In 1966 he announced that he had founded a new religion called the League of Spiritual Discovery, whose followers would spend an hour every day smoking marijuana and devote Sundays to taking LSD. In 1970 he was sentenced to fifteen years' imprisonment, but escaped with help from a group called the Weathermen.

In 1994 Leary managed to get himself arrested for smoking a cigarette in an airport as a protest against political correctness. As he was led away he said,

'Envy me, man, I bet you wish that at seventy-three years old you'll be banned for being a threat to public morals.' In his seventies he admitted the onset of senility but refused to see it as something negative, commenting, 'Senility is wasted on the old. For me it's a thrilling adventure.' He considered having his head cryogenically frozen after his death, but changed his mind after deciding that cryogenicists 'have no sense of humour. I was worried I would wake up in fifty years surrounded by people with clipboards.' In 1995 he was diagnosed as having cancer and planned a public suicide on the Internet. In fact he died peacefully in 1996. His last words were, 'Why not? Yeah.'

These experiences led to the perennial mystical preoccupation with love, peace and the mysteries of life. For a whole generation, the doors to altered states of consciousness were suddenly flung open. In the face of the decline of the influence of orthodox religions, individualistic and heretical mysticism once more presented the possibility of life having spiritual meaning. This awakening prepared the ground for the massive influx of Eastern mystical philosophy of recent years.

The chemist Albert Hofmann discovered the psychedelic drug LSD by accident in 1943, and was astonished by its effects on consciousness. He wrote: 'With my eyes closed, fantastic pictures of extraordinary plasticity and intensive colour seemed to surge towards me. . . . My power of observation was unimpaired. Occasionally I felt as if I were out of my body. I thought I had died. My ego seemed suspended somewhere in space, from where I saw my dead body lying on a sofa.'

Alan Watts, the mystic and author who played an important role in popularizing Eastern mystical ideas in the West, wrote of his experiences of LSD in a way that is directly comparable to the Taoists' experience of *wu wei*. He is no longer a 'doer'. The experiencer and the experience have become one and he has ceased to exist: 'I was no longer a detached observer, a little man inside my own head. I was the sensations, so much so that there was nothing left of me, the observing ego, except the series of sensations which happened – not to me, but just happened – moment by moment, one after the other. . . .'

In *The Doors of Perception*, written in 1954, the author and mystic Aldous Huxley recorded his experiments with the hallucinogen mescalin, a drug prepared from peyote cactus. He describes with mystical wonder the ordinary world around him coming to life. Simply looking at a chair, he is transported: 'I spent many minutes – or was it centuries – not merely gazing at those bamboo legs, but actually *being* them – or rather being myself in them; or, to be still more accurate . . . being my Not-self in the Not-self which was the chair.'

Huxley was so moved by his psychedelic experiences that he chose to take LSD on his deathbed to ease his passage to the world beyond. Author of *The Perennial Philosophy*, an important study of mysticism, Huxley had a comprehensive knowledge of the world's mystical traditions, and he felt that on LSD he was making the same transcendental inner journey as the great sages and saints. To understand his experience, he turned to familiar religious terminology:

> *Words like Grace and Transfiguration came to mind, and this is of course what, amongst other things, they stood for. My eye travelled from the rose to the carnation, and from that feathery incandescence to the smooth scrolls of sentient amethyst which were the iris. The Beatific Vision – for the first time I understood, not on a verbal level, not by inchoate hints or at a distance, but precisely and completely. . . .*

Before LSD was made illegal Timothy Leary and his associates had given out tens of thousands of free doses. The 60s psychedelic movement made Eastern mysticism very fashionable.

DRUG USE AND ABUSE

The 1990s have seen a resurgence of psychedelic mysticism. People dance wildly from dusk to dawn to an insistent trance-inducing beat under the influence of a drug appropriately named ecstasy – just as if they were partaking in some primal pagan shamanic rite. There is, however, an important difference. In the rituals of the primal peoples there is a clear awareness that they are partaking in a sacred event, and the whole of their experience is shaped by this intention. For many modern 'recreational' drug users this is not the case, and the results can be quite different.

Whilst it is undoubtedly true that countless ecstasy users, for example, enter profound altered states and find themselves overwhelmed by an all-embracing love of life, the lack of a context within which to understand this experience can potentially lead to confusion and drug abuse. The ancients did not use psychedelic plants to 'escape' from anything, but to gain entrance to what they knew to be a potentially dangerous spiritual dimension. They were ritually prepared and purified, and were initiated by wiser and more experienced figures. The use of hallucinogens has exploded into our culture without any of this understanding and support.

Despite this, an extraordinary number of people do spontaneously enter spiritually altered states. The psychedelic experience is so fascinating that all desire and discontent is suspended in child-like wonder. The very freshness of perception which is chemically engendered can bring the user completely into the fullness of the present moment, and there, like all mystics, he finds a richness beyond his dreams. Habitual use, however, can dull this freshness, and what was once a way of entering mystical rapture becomes an escapist habit.

Psychedelic drug-taking can be an important introduction to the mystical realms, but unless it leads to a genuine spiritual transformation it is only an enticing day trip to heaven from which the mystic must return. Such experiences have led many psychedelic experimenters to explore other mystical practices to find a way of becoming a resident rather than a holidaymaker in these altered states of awareness. As Ram Dass's guru Neem Karoli Baba puts it, 'LSD allows you to come into the room and bow before Christ, but after two hours you must leave. The best medicine is to love Christ.'

SCIENCE AND MYSTICISM

Ram Dass, William James and other psychologists who explored consciousness with psychedelic drugs all regarded themselves as scientists. Psychology has often been seen as on the fringe of orthodox science because of its concern with the mysteries of consciousness. Some of its most illustrious figures, such as Carl Jung, became so profoundly mystical that they had to fight to avoid being branded scientific heretics. Orthodox science sees itself as the antithesis of spirituality, yet all its great pioneers have been deeply mystical. Even in the twentieth century, when science has generally been regarded as a wholly materialist philosophy, the greatest scientists, such as Albert Einstein, have found in their work a source of mystic wonder that does not need the context of a religious tradition.

SIR ISAAC NEWTON

The seventeenth-century English scientist Sir Isaac Newton discovered the Law of Universal Gravitation, and was the most influential scientist before Einstein. What is less well known is that he was also an alchemist and astrologer who studied the Kabbala and the mystical works of the ancient Egyptian sage Hermes. Newton made copies of many alchemical texts, even copying out obscure alchemical poems. A deeply spiritual man, he was profoundly preoccupied by the search for the Oneness of God and for the divine Unity revealed in nature. He believed in the ancient wisdom concealed in myth, and was confident that he himself had discovered the true philosophy behind mythology. Newton's mystical writings far outnumber his scientific ones. Towards the end of his life he described himself as 'a boy playing on the seashore, and diverting myself in now and then finding a smoother pebble or a prettier shell than ordinary, whilst the great ocean of truth lay all undiscovered before me'.

Science has had to fight religious bigotry in order to establish itself as the new faith of the modern world, but it has a great deal in common with mysticism. Both adopt an experimental approach to life. Neither accepts blind faith, but seeks empirical proof. Science is engaged in finding the simple universal laws that govern the particulars of our complex reality. The mystics seek to experience directly the universal oneness which underlies everything.

The founding fathers of science all saw themselves as mystics. The ancient Greek proto-scientists such as Pythagoras and Archimedes were all initiates of the Mystery Schools. Figures such as Giordano Bruno and Leonardo da Vinci embodied the ideal of the Renaissance Man, who was both scientist and sage. Many of the Sufis were fascinated by science: the poet Omar Khayyám, for instance, who was a great mathematician. The physicist Isaac Newton thought his mystical work on alchemy and astrology far more significant than his scientific theories.

Many great scientists received their insights through mystical revelation. John Dee, the Elizabethan mathematician, talked to angels. The great seventeenth-century mathematician René Descartes received his 'rational' philosophical method from an angel in a dream. In the eighteenth century Emanuel Swedenborg, who amongst other great achievements developed the nebula theory of galaxies, claimed to have been speaking to angelic beings for years and to have been taken to heaven many times. The nineteenth-century chemist

The experience of beauty is the discovery of unity in variety.

SAMUEL TAYLOR COLERIDGE
Poet, opium-taker and mystical Platonist

JOHN DEE

Queen Elizabeth I's personal astrologer, whom she referred to as her 'philosopher', was the enigmatic John Dee (1527–1608). He was a brilliant mathematician and the first person to translate the compete works of Euclid into English. Dr Dee owned the greatest library in England. His home became almost a third university to rival Oxford and Cambridge, and he was visited by scholars from all over Europe. Like other great scientist of his day, such as Kepler, he saw no contradiction between being a scientist and casting horoscopes. His circle of associates included many illustrious Elizabethans including the mystic poet John Donne and the explorer Sir Walter Raleigh.

Dee worked closely with the psychic Edward Kelly, who channelled a complex series of magical letters which they called 'Enochian' and believed to be the language of the angels. His sessions with Kelly were marked by an atmosphere of devout piety. Dee believed that prayer was a key which could unlock the secrets of everything. Although widely respected by the court of Elizabeth, he suffered persecution from local villagers. They burnt his house to the ground, fearing that the mathematical symbols found there were the works of the devil. When James I came to the throne Dee found himself out of favour with the court too, and died isolated and ignored.

Friedrich Kekulé discovered the formula for benzene through a vision of a snake devouring its own tail. Georg Cantor, who developed number theory and explored concepts such as 'absolute zero' and 'absolute infinity', was institutionalized in psychiatric hospitals where he experienced visions of God and angels, which he 'converted' into mathematical formulae.

The seventeenth-century mathematician Blaise Pascal had an overwhelming mystical revelation which changed the whole course of his life. He wrote afterwards: 'Such secrets have been revealed to me that all I have written now appears of little value.' After his death a description of his ecstatic experience was found permanently sewn into his jacket, near to his heart. It read: 'From 10.30 to 12.30 Fire! Absolute certainty, beyond reason. Joy. Peace. Forgetfulness of the world and everything but God. Joy! Joy! Joy! Tears of Joy!'

Science, like religion, has in many ways become dry, institutionalized and dogmatic; but at its heart are great men and women who have been moved by a mystical sense of wonder at the richness of the world. The marine biologist Jacques Cousteau enthused:

Apache dancers from Mescalero perform a ritual in full ceremonial costume. Ecstatic dance is an ancient pathway to the mystical experience.

TEILHARD DE CHARDIN

Pierre Teilhard de Chardin (1881–1955) was a French Jesuit priest and scientist who spent much of his life in China. None of his writings received the approval of the Catholic Church, and so were not published until after his death. Exiled from France by the Church for his heretical ideas, he travelled to sites of geological and paleontological interest, developing his ideas about humankind's place in the universe. He saw his work as revealing the unity underlying religion, science, spirit and matter, and saw life as a process of evolution: with man, he felt, evolution had at last become conscious of itself. He believed that future evolution was in man's hands and that, without our strenuous and immediate cooperation, evolution on this planet and life itself might come to an end.

In his most famous work, *The Phenomenon of Man*, Teilhard de Chardin wrote: 'Fuller being is closer union. Union can only increase through an increase in consciousness, that is to say in vision. And that, doubtless, is why the history of the living world can be summarised as the elaboration of ever more perfect eyes within a cosmos in which there is always something more to see.' Today, Teilhard de Chardin is a spiritual and philosophical inspiration to many in the Green Movement.

The exhilarating quest for discovery, the search to find what magic lies beyond the stars and inside the atom, is at once wonderfully insatiable and wonderfully satisfying. We cannot find happiness in contemplating ourselves; but we can find it in contemplating infinity. Reaching out, with our imaginations, towards its majesty, it will in turn embrace us and inspire us.

THE BEING OF LIGHT

Albert Einstein said, 'I want to know God's thoughts . . . the rest are details.' From childhood, he wondered what it would be like to *be* light. His scientific discoveries beautifully complement the paradoxical spiritual insights of the mystics. The mystics say that time and space are illusions. Einstein has scientifically shown that this is true. If we could move at the speed of light, these fundamental dimensions would cease to exist. Science teaches that from light's point of view

The Whirling Dervishes were a sect established by the Sufi mystic Jalal u Din Rumi. Sufi dancers whirl in imitation of the planets orbiting around the sun, before collapsing in ecstacy.

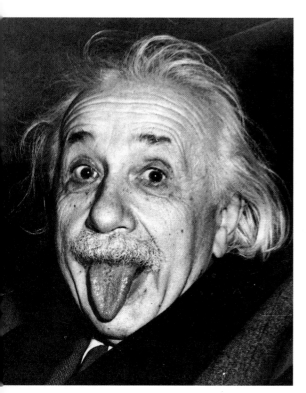

Albert Einstein, like many mystics before him, glimpsed a world where time and space simply disappear. His eccentricity and genius have made him into a modern icon.

there is no space and no time, just as the mystics teach that from God's perspective there is only oneness and eternity.

The mystics talk of the ultimate reality as the 'All and Nothing', using paradoxical phrases such as 'The Clear Light of the Void' and 'The Dazzling Darkness'. Science teaches if there were to be only pure light with nothing for it to illuminate, it would paradoxically be totally dark. Like God who cannot be seen, yet is everywhere bringing all things into existence, light reveals everything, yet is itself invisible.

Modern physics has wrestled with the paradox that light sometimes appears as made up of particles and sometimes as a wave, depending on the way the experiment is set up. This is directly comparable to the mystic's observations about consciousness. From the perspective of our normal awareness each individual is a discrete *particle* of consciousness that we experience as 'you' and 'me'. But from the sublime perspective of the mystics, there is only one consciousness and individuals are no more than *waves* rising and falling on this one ocean of being. When a mystic experiences pure consciousness he ceases to experience himself as a distinct 'particle' of consciousness, and knows himself to be a 'wave' – a transitory disturbance on the Sea of God that is his ultimate and only true identity. There are waves, but they are wholly made up of the sea. The mystic ceases to focus on the objects which light reveals, and is aware of the one light which reveals them. He turns his attention from the contents of consciousness, and focuses on consciousness Itself – the sense of 'I AM'. He *sees the light*. He is enlightened.

From its earliest beginnings in the Greek Mystery Schools to the amazing modern insights of Albert Einstein, science has always been a source of mystical wonder. Einstein wrote:

The most important function of science is to awaken the cosmic religious feeling and keep it alive. . . . It is very difficult to explain this feeling to anyone who is entirely without it. The individual feels the nothingness of human desires and aims and the sublimity and marvellous order which reveal themselves both in nature and in the world of thought. He looks upon individual existence as a sort of prison and wants to experience the universe as a single significant whole.

A NATURAL AND PERENNIAL EXPERIENCE

Whatever the method used to attain mystical experiences, whether inside or outside of a spiritual tradition, the visions received unmistakably speak of the same direct insight into the mystery of life. Apart from the language used, the accounts of all the mystics are so similar that if we did not know who was speaking it would be hard to say what tradition a particular visionary belonged to, or what method or practice was being employed. From the earliest shamans to the modern psychedelic mystics, all these remarkable men and women speak of a common realization. It is clear that the mystical experience is a natural state of consciousness, available to everyone regardless of their culture or conditions. It is not a religious experience, it is a human experience. It is simply the discovery of the truth.

Alan Watts is a twentieth-century writer on Eastern mysticism. Immersed in the beauty of a starlit garden whilst under the influence of LSD, he captures the awe and wonder of all the mystics who experience the perennial revelation of an intelligent love permeating the universe:

> *Feeling then, not that I was drugged but that I was in an unusual degree open to reality, I tried to discern the meaning, the inner character of the dancing pattern which constituted both myself and the garden, and the whole dome of the night with its coloured stars. All at once it became obvious that the whole thing was love-play, where love means everything that the word can mean, a spectrum ranging from the red of erotic delight, through the green of human endearment, to the violet of divine charity, from Freud's libido to Dante's 'love that moves the sun and other stars'. All were so many colours issuing from a single white light, and, what was more, this single source was not just love as we ordinarily understand it: it was also intelligence. I could see that the intricate organisation both of the plants and of my own nervous system, alike symphonies of branching complexity, were not just manifestations of intelligence. It was rather that the pattern itself is intelligence and is love.*

Make your eye single and you will be full of light.

JESUS

11

THE ESSENCE OF MYSTICISM

◆

I AM,
can be spoken by no creature,
but by God alone.
I must become God,
and God must become me,
so completely,
that we share the same 'I' eternally.
Our truest 'I'
is
God.

MEISTER ECKHART
Fourteenth-century Christian mystic

'*I WENT IN SEARCH* of myself' declared the Greek philosopher Heraclitus in the fifth century BC. This is the start of the mystical quest – the simple question 'Who am I?' The mystic turns his attention away from his perceptions, and goes in search of the perceiver. He stops looking to the world for answers to the mysteries of life, and begins instead to look within to explore his own identity. What does he find? The mystical experience reveals to him his true nature – an immortal soul that will not decay and die like his physical body; a permanent spiritual essence, beyond the ever-changing flux of thoughts and emotions that he took to be his 'self'. 'Ecstasy' means 'to stand outside'; the mystic experiences the ecstatic state of standing outside of his normal awareness of himself, and discovers that he is more than he had ever imagined.

Unlike the personality, which experiences itself as a separate entity, distinct from others and the rest of life, the soul knows itself to be a part of the whole, intimately connected to everyone and everything. When the mystic realizes his true nature he does not discover something private and personal, but rather something shared by all. He is a spark of the one fire. The path of the mystic is to find and then feed this spark, until it burns up his separate ego.

The mystic's discovery of the higher Self is only a step on a greater journey. The soul is only real in so far as it is a connection between the separate personality and God. In the *Upanishads* it says: 'There is a bridge between time and eternity; this bridge is *Atman* – the Higher Self.' When this bridge is crossed and the mystic experiences the vision of unity, the bridge itself is seen as an illusion. Just like a person who discovers that the moon does not shine by its own light, but only by reflecting the sun, the mystic discovers that the soul is only a reflection of the light of God. Ultimately he has no identity except as divinity. This is why Jesus claimed, 'I and my Father are One', and al-Hallaj declared, 'I am God.'

In established Jewish, Christian and Islamic religion, to claim to be one with God is seen as blasphemous. Both Jesus and al-Hallaj were crucified by the religious authorities of their day for uttering such a heresy. But this has not stopped mystics from within these faiths discovering this truth for themselves. 'My me is God, nor do I recognise any other me except my God Himself,' declared St Catherine of Genoa. One day a neighbour knocked on the door of Bayazid of

The moon has no light of its own, but reflects the light of the sun. The mystic comes to realise that the self is only a reflection of the Self.

This is to be understood by the heart, there is no separateness at all.

The Upanishads

133

Bistun's door and shouted, 'Is Bayazid here?' The Sufi saint replied from inside, 'Is anybody here except God?'

Plotinus paradoxically describes this spiritual journey as 'a flight from the solitary to the solitary'. It is a voyage from 'alone' to 'all-one'. With this realization, there is no longer any sense of 'other': everything is the manifestation of the one consciousness. The lover of God merges with his 'beloved' and becomes love itself. The knower of truth merges with the known and becomes knowledge. There is no longer a subject (the searching mystic) and an object (the searched for God) – there is only a simple state of indescribable completeness. Meister Eckhart says: 'The knower and the known are one. Simple people imagine that they should see God as if He stood there and they here. This is not so. God and I, we are one in knowledge.'

When the mystic reaches the end of his search for himself, he finds he has no self. He is nothing, yet paradoxically he is everything. In the first century, when the Romans sacked the Jewish Temple in Jerusalem, they were astounded to find that the Holy of Holies, the sanctuary at its centre, was empty of all images and icons. In the same way, when the mystic finds the temple of his soul he discovers in it the splendour of emptiness. The Buddhists call this experience 'enlightenment'. Like a drop of water dissolving back into the mighty sea, the individual soul returns to the primal source.

This metaphor has filled some students of mysticism with horror. It can sound like total annihilation – not a very appealing prospect – but this is a misunderstanding. The personal self cannot cease to be, because in truth it never existed – it was merely a transitory illusion. An enlightened soul is not lost in the overwhelming vastness of the ocean of being – it knows that there has only ever been the ocean. When the Buddha was asked if a person who attains enlightenment could still be said to exist, he replied, 'It would be wrong to say he does, and it would be wrong to say he does not.' The separate self is like a wave upon the sea which, although distinct, is no more than a disturbance on the surface of the waters.

Some 1400 years ago in China, the Empress Wu became fascinated with the relationship between the essential Oneness and the apparent multiplicity of life. She asked the sage Fa Tsang if he could give a simple practical demonstration to help her understand. Fa Tsang arranged one of the palace rooms so that eight large mirrors stood at the eight points of the compass. He then placed a further mirror on the floor, and another on the ceiling. A candle was suspended in the centre of the room, and the Empress was invited in. Fa Tsang then lit the candle and the room was filled with the splendour of reflected light. The Empress Wu was awed and overcome by the beauty of this vision. 'You see, your majesty,' said Fa Tsang. 'This is the one and the many. The candle is the One Consciousness of God, and the reflections are the many individual consciousnesses of his creation.' The soul is a reflection of One Consciousness. In a sense it is individual, yet it could not be said to exist independently. Indeed, the source and the reflection are the same light.

THE MYSTICAL PATH

Few seekers immediately transcend their sense of separateness and permanently merge with God. Most undergo a lengthy and challenging learning process which will transform their lives. For all mystics who have yet to arrive at the maturity of final enlightenment, the ecstasy of the sudden transcendental vision is short-lived. Jung recorded his despondency as his mystical elation faded:

Usually the visions lasted for about an hour; then I would fall asleep again. By the time morning drew near, I would feel: Now grey morning is coming again; now comes the grey world with its boxes! What idiocy, what hideous nonsense! Those inner states were so fantastically beautiful that by comparison the world appeared downright ridiculous.

The mystic experience leaves a legacy, however – a memory of freedom. The twentieth-century sage Gurdjieff says, 'Until we know we are in prison there is no hope of escape.' The mystic has been shown beyond doubt that he is a prisoner of his own personality. The more he tastes the sweetness of transcending his limited self, the more he thirsts for complete release. He starts consciously to cultivate an awareness of his true nature, and becomes a pilgrim on the spiritual path.

Sengstan, the third Zen Patriarch, said: 'The Great Way is easy to follow, for those who have no preferences.' For the rest of us, however, who are forever wanting this and not that, seeking pleasure but not pain, impatiently rushing into the future and holding on to the past – for those of us without an enlightened equanimity, the Great Way is far from easy. In contrast to the simple immediacy of the transcendental vision, the mystic path is fraught with trials and tribulations. It is pictured as a spiral, a maze or a labyrinth, through which the mystic must manoeuvre; now lost, now found, until as if by chance arriving at the centre. Or it is the holy mountain he must climb: step by step over difficult and dangerous terrain, until he arrives at the astonishing view from the summit.

One in All, All in One. When this is realised, no more worry about not being perfect.

SENGSTAN
Third Zen Patriarch

JUNG'S DREAM

Carl Jung, one of the founding fathers of psychology, reported an extraordinary dream in which he found himself in a small chapel. He was surprised to see on the altar, not a crucifix or statue of the Virgin Mary, but a yogi sitting cross-legged in the lotus position with his eyes closed in meditation. Looking more closely, he realized with 'profound fright' that this still and silent yogi had Jung's own face. He awoke with the mystic realization that whilst this deeper Self remained asleep the personality of Jung would exist, but when the yogi awoke then his personality would cease to be.

Although Jung was keen to portray himself as a scientist, some have argued that concepts such as the 'collective unconscious' and his theory of archetypes owe as much to nineteenth-century occultism and neo-paganism as they do to natural science, and that Jung was in effect founding a type of new religion modelled on the teachings of the ancient Mystery Schools. Certainly Jung was greatly influenced by the Gnostics and alchemy, and himself wrote a Gnostic work called *Seven Sermons for the Dead* – he never published it for fear of undermining his reputation, but circulated it privately to such close friends as the novelist Herman Hesse.

At every turn of the path the mystic is confronted with his own separate self. The light of the mystic experience shows up the darkness of his ego, which he must acknowledge and overcome. As the sixteenth-century Christian mystic Fénelon said:

> *As the light grows, we see ourselves to be worse than we thought. We are amazed at our former blindness as we see issuing from our heart a whole swarm of shameful feelings, like filthy reptiles crawling from a hidden cave. But we must be neither amazed nor disturbed. We are not worse than we were; on the contrary we are better. But while our faults diminish, the light we see them by waxes brighter, and we are filled with horror.*

Although the mystic's initiatory transcendental experiences brought the world to life, his subsequent spiritual journey may seem to be killing it. As he disengages himself from the dramas of his personal life, it appears as if the colour has drained out of things. Familiar activities that once excited his interest now leave him cold. He may experience the loneliness and spiritual isolation which St John of the Cross called 'The Dark Night of the Soul'. He is no longer of this world, yet not fully of God either. He may feel apart from his culture or ostracized by others who see him as eccentric or neurotic, for he is now consumed with a mystical obsession for union with God.

The twentieth-century Hindu sage Radhakrishnan describes spiritual development as a 'growth in impersonality'. All the techniques used by mystics from different traditions are methods of transcending the personality and finding the impersonal Self. Sai Baba teaches that 'The aim of all religion is to kill the false I, so that the real, the Lord, will reign.' He suggests that this is the deeper meaning of the Christian symbol of the Cross – it represents an 'I' that has been crossed out. The separate self must die, so that the higher Self may come to life. This is why in the mystical traditions the ego is often seen as the enemy. 'If you have never seen the devil, take a look at your own self,' admonishes the Sufi saint Rumi.

The passionate desire to be free from bondage to the false 'I' has led to many kinds of self-denial and asceticism. These have sometimes taken the extreme form of self-flagellation and other sorts of bodily torture, but such practices are universally condemned by mature mystics, who choose healthier paths. The mystic may seek to purify himself of desire by fasting, or cleanse himself in symbolical rituals like baptism. He may undertake pilgrimages as a physical enactment of his inner journey to God. He may frequent sacred sites, temples or places of great natural beauty where worship has been undertaken for thousands of years and which have become charged with spiritual power.

Carl Jung was the founder of depth psychology. His researches into the ancient gnostics and Mystery School initiates profoundly influenced his therapeutic technique.

ST JOHN OF THE CROSS

John de Yepes was born in 1542 near Avila, and became Spain's most notable mystic. He entered the Carmelite order in 1563 and became a priest four years later. The following year, however, adopting the name John of the Cross, he took vows in the reformed Discalced Carmelite order founded by the mystic St Teresa of Avila. He was twice kidnapped by the Calced Carmelites, whom he and Teresa wanted to reform. During his second imprisonment, in 1577–8, he wrote the classic mystical text *The Dark Night of the Soul*. After his escape he became a vicar and prior, before being officially disgraced and stripped of all his offices in 1591, just before his death. His works, which have sometimes been suppressed, describe the spiritual road that will lead to perfect union with God. For John, God is like a fire and man like a cold, damp log. Through a process of spiritual transformation, man can take on the light of God's wisdom and the heat of his love.

He may set the world aside and become a hermit, or live in the cloistered environment of a monastery, so that he will not be distracted by worldly concerns. The mystic may choose to lose himself in love by selflessly serving others. He may still his mind in prayer and meditation to find the unity of silence.

The interior life of human beings consists of thoughts and feelings, and the mystics use both head and heart to lead them to God. The philosopher's path is to use his mind to transcend the mind. The word 'intelligence' means literally 'to reach between'. The intellect reaches between the multiplicity of the world and the Oneness of God, connecting them and uniting them. In the stillness of contemplation, rather than the dialectic of rational argument, the mystic philosopher awakens his innate knowledge which is richer and more complete than if had read a whole library of books. Jacob Boehme claimed to learn more in a quarter of an hour of mystical experience than many years at university, for he 'saw and knew the Being of all Beings'.

The path of the devotee is to open the heart to love. Whilst the

GURDJIEFF AND OUSPENSKY

George Gurdjieff was a charismatic Armenian rascal sage born in the 1870s. In his twenties, accompanied by a band of friends who called themselves 'Seekers after Truth', he set off towards the East, visiting amongst other places central Asia and Tibet. During his remarkable adventures he studied with many spiritual masters and was influenced by Sufism. On his return he set up an esoteric school in Russia, but fled to America during the turmoil surrounding the 1917 Revolution. In the 1920s and 1930s he attracted many rich and famous people to his teachings. Gurdjieff saw his goal as 'waking man up so that he does not sleep walk through life'. He set out to 'destroy, mercilessly and without any compromises whatsoever, all beliefs and views about everything

existing in the world', and taught a method of self-remembering through which the student could become free from his habitual personality.

Gurdjieff's most famous student was the Russian philosopher and mystic P. D. Ouspensky. Towards the end of his life Ouspensky addressed a large meeting of his students in London. He stumbled on to the platform, clearly very drunk, and simply announced that everyone should go away and work things out for themselves because there had never been a 'system' to follow. The meeting split into those who regarded this statement as an admission that he had nothing to teach, and those who felt this was the final teaching of their master.

THE ESSENCE OF MYSTICISM

philosophers see the divine as an absolute impersonal oneness, such mystics approach God more like a person with whom they can share an intimate relationship – a divine devotional love affair in which they may lose themselves in their beloved. Love unites all things; through it we transcend the division of self and other. As Sri Nisargadatta puts it, 'Love is the bridge between spirit and matter.'

The great mystics walk both the path of knowledge and the path of love. They transcend the division of head and heart in the experience of knowing God and therefore being love – for to experience the oneness of life is also to experience an all-embracing, unconditional compassion for the whole of creation. Head and heart are like the two legs with which we walk – they work together to carry us to our eternal home. Meister Eckhart wrote: 'Up then noble soul! Put on thy jumping shoes, which are intellect and love, and overleap the worship of thy mental powers, overleap thine understanding, and spring into the heart of God.'

BEYOND THE MYSTIC PATH

The path, however, is not the destination, and the seeker must be careful not to confuse the two. He will become trapped in anything that sustains his separate self, including spirituality. The ego likes to see itself as a pious devotee, a wise philosopher, a selfless servant, a disciplined ascetic. But it only wants to *appear* to be these things. The ego cannot seek its own annihilation, but willingly embraces the inflated idea of being a 'special person' – a seeker after truth. The mystic wrestles constantly with this dilemma, which threatens to make all his spiritual practices self-enlarging, not self-diminishing. The path is only a means to an end, and the mystic must avoid becoming so enamoured with the techniques he is using to liberate himself that he forgets their purpose; he must not honour his spiritual disciplines so rigorously that they fail to set him free.

There is a story of two Buddhist monks who had taken many vows, including never to look at a woman. One day they were walking home towards their monastery when they came to a fast-flowing river. On the banks of the river stood a young girl who was too frightened to try to cross the raging torrent. One of the monks, a youthful novice, dutifully turned his eyes away and began to wade across. But the other monk, his elderly teacher, walked over to the girl, lifted her upon his shoulders and carried her across to the other side. Some hours afterwards, as the monks continued their silent journey home, the young novice could contain himself no longer and exclaimed: 'I don't under-

The Supreme Wisdom is the Oneness of things; the Supreme Compassion is the Manyness of things.

D. T. SUZUKI
Zen master

stand, master. We have taken a solemn vow not to look at a woman, let alone pick one up and carry her. How could you betray your holy orders?'

'What?' replied the old master. 'Are you still carrying that young woman? I put her down on the bank of the river.'

Although many mystics choose to live within rigid rules of conduct, this is a means to an end, not an end in itself. It is not a code to be blindly obeyed but a containment of the separate self, to allow the true Self to be free. When he experiences his Self, the mystic naturally and spontaneously acts for the best and needs no dogmatic regulations. The Christian St Augustine of Hippo wrote: 'Love and do what you will.' In the *Bhagavad Gita* the god Krishna declares to his pupil Arjuna, 'I have thus revealed to you the Truth, the deepest of all secrets; meditate on it, then do whatever you want.' If the mystic understanding is genuinely grasped, the mystic cannot contravene it. If he truly loves all, how can he seek to harm? If he truly understands that desire leads to bondage, how can he follow his personal will? He does not need to try to do good – he is goodness. Genuine spirituality does not lie in obeying the rules of religion, or in being a good meditator or a disciplined ascetic. It lies only in dispelling the illusion of being a separate self.

THE SIMPLE TRUTH

Absence of attachment to sense-objects is liberation; desire for sense-objects is bondage. Understand this fact, and then do as you please.

ASHTAVAKRA GITA
Hindu scripture

When we totally abandon the illusion of being a separate self, we will have found spiritual freedom: freedom from pride – for there is no one to be proud, and no one to compare with; freedom from judgment – because there is no one to judge and no one to be judged; freedom from fear – for there is nothing to lose and nothing to gain; freedom from anxiety – for there is nowhere to go and no one to go there; freedom, in short, from the sufferings of life. In a characteristically challenging fashion, the Hindu master Sri Nisargadatta sums up the radical message of the mystics: 'You have squeezed yourself into the span of a lifetime and the volume of a body, and thus created the innumerable conflicts of life and death. Have your being outside this body of birth and death, and all your problems will be solved. They exist because you believe yourself born to die. Undeceive yourself and be free. You are not a person.'

12

LIVING MYSTICISM

❖

Is it wonderful that I should be immortal? as everyone is immortal.
I know it is wonderful – but my eyesight is equally wonderful,
and how I was conceived in my mother's womb is equally wonderful;
And passed from a babe, in the creeping trance
of a couple of summers and winters, to articulate and walk –
all this is equally wonderful.
And that my Soul embraces you this hour,
and we affect each other without seeing each other,
and never perhaps to see each other, is every bit as wonderful.
And that I can think such thoughts as these is just as wonderful;
And that I can remind you,
and you think them and know them to be true
is equally wonderful.

WALT WHITMAN
Mystic poet

The Oudja Eye *is a hieroglyph of the divine light imprisoned in matter. The right eye is the sun that sees into eternity, the left is the moon that sees into the world of time and change.*

MYSTICISM is not just for saints and sages. All of life is the mystic path, and we are all knowing or unknowing pilgrims. Every one of us is a drop from the one ocean of God. Whilst the grand visions of the mystics may seem exotic and other-worldly, most of us have at some time or other been consumed by wonder – perhaps watching light dancing on the sea or the splendour of the setting sun, seeing the familiar face of a loved one, or under the transforming impact of loss and grief. Starting like an embryo in the womb of our awareness, such experiences are the stirrings of mystical insight.

Whether it be a psychedelically inspired shaman, an ancient initiate of the Mystery Schools, a Christian nun or a Buddhist monk – all have been human like the rest of us, and all have sought meaning in this sometimes strange and confusing world. We all face the same fundamental questions and search for the same fundamental answers. We all have this human life as an opportunity for spiritual awakening. The Zen master Echu says: 'It is a rare privilege to be born human, as we happen to be. If we do not achieve enlightenment in this life, when do we expect to achieve it?'

We live at a unique moment in history, when for the first time the great mystical traditions of the world are readily accessible, meeting and interacting to reveal new possibilities. Today, we are not limited by geography and culture in the path we choose. We may follow any number of ways to suit our own needs, or take elements from many different traditions. It does not matter which mystic path we walk, only that we travel. What fires our mind or touches our heart is a personal matter. The danger today is of being overwhelmed by choice. How can we choose one way amongst so many?

The mystics answer that we each have a soul, which at first we experience as a spiritual guide or 'genius', and this alone can lead us on our own unique spiritual journey. We are in search of our own Self, so only our Self can ultimately be our guide. In his allegorical epic poem *The Divine Comedy*, the thirteenth-century poet Dante imagines himself wandering lost in Purgatory. Here he meets his dead teacher, the mystic alchemist Brunetto Lantini, who advises him, 'Follow but thy star, and thou cannot fail to win glorious heaven.' Only our own star can light our way. There are no rules to follow in choosing a spiritual path – only to follow our own heart. The modern Mexican shaman Don Juan advised his pupil Carlos Casteneda: 'Look at every path closely and deliberately. Try it as many times as you think necessary. Then ask yourself, and yourself alone, one question. Does this path have a heart? If it does, the path is good; if it doesn't, it is of no use.'

We do not have to follow any spiritual tradition, however, to open ourselves to the mystic vision – only to change the way we see our life. Done with the right intention, any activity in life can become a spiritual practice through which we may transcend our separate self. What are the simple changes we can make in the way we approach our life that can transform it into an adventure into consciousness?

LIVING WITH LOVE

Opening the heart to love is the central mystic teaching. This is something we can experience in every moment of our lives. Most people have experienced the unifying power of love. Lovers lose themselves in their love for one another. In physical love, two bodies become one. The boundaries of the separate self are dissolved and we enter the bliss of union. Socrates, relating the teachings of his mentor the prophetess Diotima, says that such love of another person is a pathway into Love itself, which can lead from the particular to the universal – from love for one person to Love for all.

DON JUAN AND CARLOS CASTANEDA

The American anthropologist Carlos Castaneda became something of a cult figure in the 1970s after his claims to have been instructed in the Yaqui Way of Knowledge by a Mexican shaman called Don Juan. Don Juan is an enigmatic teacher who led the young Carlos through various spiritual initiations, sometimes involving the use of natural psychedelic substances. He teaches: 'When you *see*, there are no familiar features in the world. Everything is new. Everything has never happened before. The world is incredible! There is really no way to talk about it.' To an ordinary man, says Don Juan, everything is a blessing or a curse, but to a Man of Knowledge everything is a challenge and an opportunity. Many people have questioned the genuineness of Castaneda's reports and whether Don Juan actually exists, but his teachings are certainly in line with the traditions of the native peoples of Mexico and the American south-west, and have had a profound influence on those seeking to understand the shamanic path to mystical knowledge.

Personal love is directed towards an object of desire – a person we wish to be with, or a thing we wish to possess. It is conditional love, because if the person or thing does not fulfil our expectations we no longer feel the love. To expand beyond limited personal love and experience the all-embracing love of God, the mystics advise us to cultivate a compassion for everyone and everything – to love for no reason and for no reward. Love is the universal force of attraction, which, like gravity, pulls all things together as one. If we can transcend our sense of separateness, we will expand beyond personal love to an unconditional compassion – becoming the One loving the All. Sri Nisargadatta says:

> *Life is love and love is life. What keeps the body together but love? What is desire but love of self? What is fear but the urge to protect? What is knowledge but the love of Truth? The means and forms may be wrong, but the motive behind is always love – love of the 'me' and 'mine'. The me and mine may be small, or may explode and embrace the universe, but love remains.*

When our 'me' and 'mine' explode and we become the universe, the mystics teach, we will love all things as a part of our self. Love is both the road to this transcendence and the destination. Only when we love all will we know the One. Only when we know the One will we be all love.

LIVING IN THE ONENESS OF THE ALL

Sai Baba says: 'All are One, and if someone believes otherwise, they are circumscribing their part in the whole and are imprisoning themselves in the part.' By circumscribing our part in the whole we alienate ourselves from the rest of existence and become a prisoner inside our own sense of self. The mystics urge us no longer to experience the world as a confusing mass of distinct and isolated people and things, but to see the Oneness which underlies everything. The modern Vietnamese Zen master Thich Nhat Hanh writes:

> *If you are a poet, you will clearly see that there is a cloud floating in this sheet of paper. Without a cloud, there will be no rain; without rain, the trees cannot grow; and without trees, we cannot make paper. If we look even more deeply, we can see the sunshine, the logger who cut the tree,*

the wheat that became his bread, and the logger's father and mother. Without all of these things, this sheet of paper cannot exist. In fact, we cannot point to one thing that is not there – time, space, the earth, the rain, the minerals in the soil, the sunshine, the cloud, the river, the heat, the mind. Everything co-exists with this sheet of paper. So we can say that the cloud and the paper 'inter-are'. We cannot just be by ourselves alone, we have to inter-be with every other thing.

The mystical vision of Oneness is revealed when we experience the totality within which the parts are so inter-related they could not be said to exist independently. Just as the liver in a human body could not exist without the brain, and the lungs could not function without the heart, so all of creation can be seen to be like one great body of the creator: each part performs its role according to its nature, yet functions as a whole.

LIVING IN THE MAGIC OF LIFE

'You are a fish swimming in an ocean of God,' says Sai Baba. The mystics encourage us always to appreciate what a magical mystery life is – to see the 'miraculous' within what we have reduced to the 'ordinary'. 'Why! who makes much of a miracle?' asked the American mystic poet Walt Whitman. 'As for me I know nothing but miracles.' When we are open to a mystical awareness, ordinary life guides us in the form of magical coincidences that Jung called 'synchronicity', which eventually become so frequent and abundant that they cease to be remarkable. Whitman wrote:

> *I find letters from God dropped in the street, and every one is signed by God's name,*
> *And I leave them where they are, for I know that others will punctually come forever and ever.*

If we have the eyes to see, the world in which we live is our guru, revealing to us deep mystic truths. The poet William Blake, for example, could stare in awe for hours at a knot in a piece of wood, amazed at the concentric rings of growth surrounding one invisible centre from which the whole branch had been produced, and immersing himself in the mystery of the creation of something from nothing.

All those who walk with God reach their destination.

SAI BABA
Modern Hindu mystic

LIVING WITH ACCEPTANCE

There is no one in the world who cannot arrive without difficulty at the most eminent perfection by fulfilling with love obscure and common duties.

JEAN PIERRE DE CAUSSADE
Christian mystic

The mystics advise us to cultivate a state of complete acceptance – to become unmoved by praise or blame, untouched by pleasure or pain, indifferent to loss or gain. This is a state not of complacent resignation, but of surrendering to God's will with equanimity. The seventeenth-century French mystic Jean Pierre de Caussade advised: 'Do what you are doing now, suffer what you are suffering now; to do all this with holiness, nothing need be changed but your heart. Sanctity consists in willing what happens to us by God's order.'

Through such acceptance we can embody a universal patience, humility and compassion, like the sixteenth-century French mystic St François de Sales who treated everyone, even the most socially insignificant person, as though they were his superior. He never rejected anyone, never refused to enter into conversation, never betrayed any sign of boredom. To those who asked him why he wasted his time in this way, he replied: 'It is God's will; it is what He requires of me; what more need I ask? While I am doing this, I am not required to do anything else. God's Holy Will is the centre from which all we do must radiate; all else is mere weariness and excitement.'

This acceptance and equanimity is not a weak passivity, but the strength that comes from transcending the separate self. There is a Burmese teaching story about a tyrant whose armies have laid waste the country. He arrives at a small village and is informed by his generals that the local population have all run away into the hills; everyone, that is, except one monk who refuses to leave his monastery. The tyrant is so enraged by such impudence that he marches over to the monastery to confront the monk.

'Don't you know who I am?' he growls. 'I could take out my sword and cut you in two without blinking an eye.'

The monk replies serenely, 'Don't you know who I am? I could stand here while you take out your sword and cut me in two, without blinking an eye.'

When we have acceptance we are no longer attached to the transitory things of this world – even our own bodily survival. As Jesus advises in the Gnostic Gospel of Thomas, we become like a 'passer-by'.

LIVING FREE FROM DESIRE

Our will is fuelled by our desires, and the mystics teach us to give up these desires and desire only what is. To transcend our separate self truly we must even abandon the desire for God or Truth or whatever name we give to our spiritual goal. Meister Eckhart wrote:

> *A man must become truly poor and as free from his own creaturely will as when he was born. And I tell you, by the eternal truth, that so long as you desire to fulfil the will of God and have any hankering after eternity and God, for just so long you are not truly poor. He alone has true spiritual poverty, who wills nothing, knows nothing, desires nothing.*

The mystics tell us to concentrate all of our desires into the one desire to know God, and then finally, as we cross the threshold of realization, to be ready to abandon this also. The Hindus imagine the separate self consumed in fire, like a corpse on a funeral pyre. The desire for God is like the stick with which the priest stokes the fire to make sure the body is completely turned to ash; when it is, the stick too is thrown into the flames.

LIVING WITH BEGINNER'S MIND

The maverick Hindu guru Neem Karoli Baba says, 'To see God everywhere you need special eyes; otherwise you cannot bear the shock.' To see with special eyes, we need only perceive the world without the distorting lenses of our theories and opinions – no matter how elevated they may be. Only then will we see things as they are. When we simply *see*, like a child sees, the world is fresh, the colours are vibrant, everything is alive. Jesus says, 'Except you become as little children, you cannot enter the kingdom of heaven.' 'The kingdom belongs to the child,' declares the Greek philosopher Heraclitus. 'If you want to know about the Tao,' suggests the Chinese master Lao Tzu, 'take a look at little children.'

To reach the maturity of spiritual enlightenment we must recapture the pristine immediacy that we experienced as little children. The mystical experience may sound strange and alien, but it is actually home. It returns us to that primal awareness that we knew even before

> *People should think less about what they ought to do, and more about what they ought to be.*
>
> **MEISTER ECKHART**
> **Christian mystic**

*In the Great Tao
There is no Yesterday,
No tomorrow,
No today.*

SENGSTAN
Third Zen Patriarch

we learned to talk; before we learned to think; before we learned to see ourselves as a separate and distinct individual. This is why Meister Eckhart says, 'God is nearer to me than I am to myself.' It is only our 'grown-up' opinions and educated beliefs that stand between us and direct intuitive knowing.

Ironically, to walk the mystic path we must stay an eternal beginner, retaining the humble ignorance, innocence and enthusiasm with which we start the quest. 'Zen mind is beginner's mind,' says master Shunryu Suzuki. The quality of awareness realized in the mystic experience has the freshness and energy of the constant novice, and only this openness can sustain us on our adventure into consciousness. St François de Sales says: 'Be patient with everyone, but above all with yourself. I mean do not be disheartened by your imperfections, but always rise up with fresh courage. There is no better means of attaining to the spiritual life than by continually beginning again.'

LIVING AN IMPERSONAL LIFE

The mystics encourage us not to seek intellectual answers to our questions, but to keep inquiring, 'Who is asking?' In one Chinese story, when an emperor asked a sage, 'Where is the Buddha?', the sage replied, 'He is not far from where your question is coming.' 'Know Your Self' was inscribed above the Oracle at Delphi in ancient Greece. This is a challenge that needs no particular talents or qualifications and which we can undertake at any moment of any day. But what is your 'self'? Words like 'soul' and *atman* can sound strange and other-worldly. What exactly are we looking for?

The mystics' answer is that we should concentrate on our essential sense of *being* – our feeling of 'I am'. In the midst of all the changes of life, this is the one thing that is permanently present: not our ever-changing thoughts and feelings; not our body, which alters as it ages; not our personality, which transforms as it develops; but our ineffable sense of our own existence. It is the only common thread which links the experiences of our life. It is our soul.

If we look closely we will find that this 'I am', although obvious, is always completely undefinable. As soon as we add to it, saying, 'I am this or that', it is no longer our permanent essence, because those qualities change and pass away. We may say something as simple as 'I am a man' or 'I am a woman', but there was a time when we were a child, and there will be a time when we are dead. We may say, 'I am of this profession or have this social role', but these qualities too are transitory. There is absolutely nothing we can say about this 'I' which unites our life. So what is it that makes it '*us*'? It is not *our* conscious-ness – it is simply *the* Consciousness. It is universal and impersonal. It is God.

LIVING IN THE HERE AND NOW

Our sense of 'I am' is the doorway to mystical truth. It is always and only here and now. It is open to us at this very moment. To pass through, the mystics teach, we must seek neither to focus on an antic-ipated future nor to dwell on the past, but rather to appreciate the fullness of this instant – for the Eternal Now is the only place in which the 'I am' can be found. Rumi says, 'The Sufi is the son of time pre-sent.' The eighteenth-century philosopher Hegel wrote, 'Spirit is immortal; with it there is no past, no future, but an essential *now*.'

We miss our simple essential nature because of our fears and desires. Such anticipation of what might be obscures what actually *is* right now. Desire is the memory of pleasure which we seek to repeat, and fear is the memory of pain which we seek to avoid. These memo-ries and the states of anticipation which they breed are like a smoke-screen dividing us from the mystical vision.

Our memories are the stories we tell ourselves about who we have been, and hence who we are, which smother our present experience of 'I am'. In this way, we obscure the soul and so believe ourselves to be an impermanent personality. To find our permanent essence we have only to change our relationship with our memories. We can have memories, but must cease to identify with them. This, the mystics tell us, is the road to peace. It means freedom from anxiety and expecta-tion about the future, pride and regret about the past. St John of the Cross wrote: 'This emptying of memory which delivers souls from much sorrow and grief and sadness, besides imperfections and sins, is in reality a great good.'

Our memories create our idea of what the world is. They initiate expectations which colour our direct perceptions of reality so greatly that they could be said to create it. The *Lankavatara Sutra*, a Buddhist scripture, says: 'When the world is surveyed by an enlightened being, he perceives that its existence is due to memory that has been accu-mulated since the beginningless past, but wrongly interpreted.' The word here translated as 'memory' literally means 'perfuming'. It is as if our personality carries with it a constant odour of all it has thought and done and been, which fouls the freshness of the pure air and pre-

*What is called good
is perfect
and what is called bad
is just as perfect*

W A L T   W H I T M A N
Modern Mystic

vents us experiencing things *'as they are'*. The Chinese translate this original Sanskrit term with symbols which signify 'habit-energy'. By having memories, but not *being* our memories, we are able to respond spontaneously and intuitively to the present moment, rather than reacting from the habits and opinions of our personality. Whilst we may learn from the past, we are free to be fresh in each new moment. Recognizing how partial our personal knowledge of the world must necessarily be, we are open to new revelations and new possibilities. By disidentifying with our memories we are able to step out of the prison of the past and into the permanent present.

WAKING UP INTO ETERNITY

For mystics, the daily events of our ordinary lives reveal great truths. From our regular experience of dreaming, for example, we know that time is not the fixed dimension it is often assumed to be. This is obvious to those who faint and are afterwards shocked to hear that they have been unconscious for only a matter of moments, yet within that time have dreamt long, extraordinary adventures. Through dreaming we experience the shifting and ephemeral nature of the personality that we take ourselves to be. Every night we enter the dream world where our sense of who we are no longer has the permanence we experience while awake. Our identity dissolves and we become like another person in a strange land.

When we are not dreaming we pass unconsciously into deep sleep, in which there is no self, no other, no time – past, present or future. This is an experience that we are compelled to seek each night, so that we may get up the next day refreshed. If we refuse to sleep, we eventually pass out – such is our need to return regularly to this timeless nothingness. But who are *we* in this state of deep sleep? In the bliss of deep sleep we regularly experience ourselves as impersonal pure Consciousness aware of nothing.

Separate consciousness arises each morning like a a wave on the great sea of being. Ramana Maharshi teaches: 'If in the process of awakening from sleep you can hold your identity, you shall indeed be awake and forever.' If we can hold our deeper identity as the whole ocean, not the particular wave, then whether asleep or awake – Consciousness simply *is*. This is enlightenment.

AN ADVENTURE INTO CONSCIOUSNESS

The mystics tell us that the answers to the great mysteries of life are waiting for anyone who seeks them. Jesus said, 'Knock and the door will open.' When the door opens we discover we are already where we need to be – right here and now. There is nothing to change. Everything is perfect just as it is. We did not need to find our 'Way', only to get out of the way – to transcend our preoccupations with our separate self and realize that God has been right next to us all along. Closer than that – God is our very Self.

This is the humour of our predicament. Each one of us is God playing a cosmic game of hide and seek with himself. We may choose to play this game by following a tradition and engaging in particular spiritual practices. But the search is wider and more embracing than a faith or practice. It is all of the life we are already living. Each moment on our journey from birth to death is an opportunity to awaken. We will be faced with many difficulties and dilemmas along the way, but we need not worry, for the life of each one of us is designed to lead us to our destination.

The mystic experience can transport us beyond our worries, fears and reactions to a place where we are simply in love with life itself, in all its variety. There is good and bad – and that is perfect. There is meaning, but it can never be expressed. There is love which can never be exhausted. There is knowledge, but no opinions. There is happiness, but for no reason. There is equanimity in the face of changing fortunes and compassion for all beings. Everything is God. Everything is the ebb and flow of the Tao – ever-changing and ever the same.

Just to catch this moment with an open heart is all it takes to transform a troubled life into an extraordinary journey of awakening. Zen master Zuigan would greet himself each morning and request of himself, 'Today please try and wake up', to which he would answer, 'Yes, indeed I will.' This awakening cannot be learned, but it is real and it is possible. This is ultimately all that the great mystics can reveal to us. The rest is only ideas and concepts – a finger pointing at the moon. The finger is not the moon. The map will never be the terrain. The Truth cannot be expressed in words. And so, as Lao Tzu says,

'Enough ideas! Ideas divide up the Whole. Following Tao in the world is as natural as a mountain stream, that becomes part of a valley brook, that becomes part of a great river, that flows to the One Sea.'

> *I knocked and the door opened –*
> *but I found I had been knocking from the inside*
>
> **RUMI**
> **Sufi Mystic**

CHRONOLOGY OF MYSTICISM

◆

2000 BC

Shamanism practised by all primal peoples.
First mystical scriptures written in ancient
Egypt.
The Vedic hymns are composed in India.
In Babylon, detailed observation of the night
sky leads to the development of astrology and
the zodiac.

1500 BC

The Pyramids are used in Egypt as centres of
mystical initiation.
The birth of the Egyptian Mystery Schools

1000 BC

The Greek shamanic Cult of Dionysus
induces mystical visions using sacred
psychedelic mushrooms.
The Jewish prophet Moses experiences
visions of God.
The wisdom of the Hindu *Vedas* is distilled
into the *Upanishads*.

900 BC

Jewish prophets add to the Books of Moses.
The Greek poet Homer composes the *Iliad*
and the *Odyssey*.

800 BC

The Greek Oracle at Delphi becomes a centre
of mysticism for the next thousand years.

700 BC

The mystical philosophy of India spreads
westwards with the semi-mythical figure
Orpheus.
The worship of one God is established in
Judaism.
The first Greek philosopher/scientists.

600 BC

A wave of individualist mystics arise as a
reaction to established religion.
Lao Tzu (b. 604 BC), Chinese sage.
Buddha (550–480 BC), Hindu heretic.
Pythagoras (581–497 BC), Greek
philosopher.
Confucius (551–497 BC), Chinese moralist.
Heraclitus (544–480 BC), Greek philosopher
who interprets the mystical wisdom of the
Upanishads into Greek.
Vardhamana (*c.* 540–*c.* 468 BC), founder of
Jainism.

500 BC

The Greek philosopher Socrates (470–399 BC) openly propounds the teachings of the Mystery Schools, but leaves nothing in writing. He is executed for heresy.

Plato (427–347 BC), re-expresses Socrates' teaching as dialogues that profoundly influence all later Western mysticism.

Aristophanes (450–387 BC), the Greek playwright, is accused of divulging the secrets of Mystery School initiation in his plays.

400 BC

Chuang Tzu (369–286 BC), Taoist sage.

Alexander the Great unites Greece, Babylon, Israel, Persia and India into one vast Greek Empire, bringing all mystical traditions into constant contact. He founds dozens of new cosmopolitan cities, including Alexandria in Egypt.

300 BC

Alexandria replaces Athens as the greatest centre of learning, with the largest library in the ancient world. It contains the largest colony of Jews outside Israel; they translate the Old Testament into Greek.

The Hindu King Asoka (269–232 BC) drives the Greeks out of India. Sickened by war, he converts to Buddhism which becomes the religion of all India. He sends Buddhist missionaries all over the known world.

200 BC

Buddhist ashrams develop in the Egyptian desert. Jewish mystics called the Essenes inhabit the same desert.

In 147 BC Greece falls to the Roman Empire.

100 BC

In 62 BC Jerusalem falls to the Roman Empire.

Cicero (106–43 BC), the Roman writer and statesman, translates the great works of Greek mystical philosophy into Latin. He is initiated into the Mystery Schools.

Philo the Jew (20 BC–AD40) continues the work of Alexandrian scholars in synthesizing Jewish and Greek mysticism.

4 BC is the probable date of the birth of Jesus.

0

St Paul brings Christianity to non-Jews.

The Gnostic Gospel of Thomas is written (c. AD50).

The New Testament Gospels of Matthew, Mark and Luke are written (c. AD70–90).

AD 100

Gnostic Christianity is at its height, with teachers in Rome, Syria, Alexandria and Palestine. Influential Gnostic sages include Valentinus (60–110) and Basilides.

Plutarch (47–120), the Roman historian, becomes priest of Apollo at Delphi.

St Clement (160–220) and his pupil Origen (185–224) are the first Christian fathers to adapt the mysticism of the Mystery Schools to Christian theology.

The catacombs under Rome are used as tombs and places of mystical initiation.

The Roman poet Apuleius writes of his initiation into the Mystery Schools.

200

Plotinus (205–270) writes the clearest exposition of Platonic philosophy as a mystical path leading to oneness.

300

Christianity becomes the religion of the now 'Holy' Roman Empire. Emperor Theodosius closes all pagan temples and schools of philosophy, and book burning begins.

St Pachomius founds the first Christian monastery c. 320.

Heretical Gnostic gospels are hidden at Nag Hammadi in Egypt.
T'ao Ch'ien, Chinese Taoist poet.

400

Rome falls to the Visigoths in 411.
Constantinople (now Istanbul) becomes the capital of the Eastern Church. Its mystical sages include Pontus and Didochus.
St Augustine (354–430), Christian theologian.

500

St Dionysius produces a synthesis of Christian theology and ancient Greek mysticism.
The Hindu scripture called the *Bhagavad Gita* is composed, not in Sanskrit but in the common tongue. From it develops the devotional cult of Krishna worship.
In 520 Bodhidharma, the twenty-eighth Indian Buddhist Patriarch, comes to China and inspires the Chan school of Buddhism that will become known in Japan as Zen. He is regarded as the first Zen Patriarch.

600

Sengstan (d. 606), third Zen Patriarch.
Muhammad experiences visions of Gabriel on Mount Hira. He is inspired to write the Qur'an and founds Islam.

700

The Arab Empire completes the destruction of Alexandria begun by Julius Caesar and the later Christians. In 712, they capture north-west India.
Sankara (788–820) founds the Advaita school of Hindu mysticism.

800

The Eastern and Western Christian Churches excommunicate each other.
Baghdad, inspired by pagan mystic philosophers who had fled from Athens,

Rome and Alexandria, becomes a great centre of learning. It establishes the first university, called the House of Wisdom.
Baghdad school of Sufism begins with Rabi'a (d. 801) and Bayazid of Bastami (d. 874)

900

The Arabs (Moors) capture Spain. Jews can mingle freely with Moors and Spain becomes a centre of Jewish mysticism.
Milarepa, the Tibetan yogi, synthesizes shamanism and Buddhism to form Tibetan Buddhism.
In 992 the Sufi master al-Hallaj is crucified for heresy.
Hai Gaon (939–1038), Babylonian Jewish mystic.

1000

Sufism is developed by Ahmad Ghazali (d. 1061) and Aym Hamadani (1098–1131).
Omar Khayyám (1027–1123), Sufi mystic, poet and mathematician.

1100

Catharism is the dominant faith in the South of France.
In 1142 Bogomils are burnt for heresy in Cologne.
St Francis of Assisi (1182–1226), founder of the order of Fransician friars, influenced by the Cathars.

1200

Eisai (1141–1215) and his pupil Dogen (1200–53) bring Zen Buddhism to Japan after visiting China, where it is further developed by Zen master Mummon (1183–1260).
Attar Farid (1142–1220), Sufi saint.
Jala ud-Din Rumi (1207–73), Sufi saint and founder of the Whirling Dervishes.
The Inquisition is set up to eradicate Catharism and thousands of Cathars are burnt

to death. Laymen are forbidden to read the Bible.

The Zohar, a Jewish mystical work, is written in Spain, where the Jewish Kabbala begins to flourish.

Islamic Sufis, Jewish Kabbalists and Christian Cathars communicate with each other in Spain and the South of France.

St Thomas Aquinas (1225–74), Christian theologian.

Abulafia (1240–91), Jewish mystic Kabbalist.

Meister Eckhart (1260–1327) inspires the German mystics called the Friends of God. He influences Mechtild of Magdeburg (1212–99), Henry Suso (1295–1365) and Jan Ruysbroek (1293–1381). Dante (1265–1321), the great Italian mystic poet, unites the mysticism of St Thomas Aquinas, Mechtild of Magdeburg and St Dionysius into a grand vision of the Absolute.

1300

By 1300 the whole of India is in Arab hands and Indian Buddhism is all but obliterated. The works of St Dionysius are translated into English by an anonymous author, who also writes *The Cloud of Unknowing*. Both works inspire a wave of English mystics including Mother Julian of Norwich (1343–1413).

Ikkyu (1394–1481), Zen master and poet.

After the fourteenth century, Sufism declines.

1400

Cardinal Nicholas of Cusa (1401–64), the last of the great German mystics. He makes a failed attempt to reconcile the Western and Eastern Churches.

Constantinople falls to the Arabs and Platonic mystics flee to the tolerant city state of Florence in Italy, where the Catholic priest Marsilio Ficino translates the lost works of Plato, Plotinus and Hermes into Latin. A New Platonic Academy is established, which includes Leonardo da Vinci (1452–1519) and Michelangelo (1475–1564), and the Renaissance begins.

Kabir and Mirabai, Indian mystic poets.

Guru Nanak (1469–1539), founder of Sikhism.

1500

In 1517 Martin Luther begins the Reformation in Germany. In 1518 he publishes the mystical ideas of the Friends of God.

Isaac Luria (1533–72) develops a new mystical Kabbala which is imported into the West by figures like John Dee (1572–1618) and Giordano Bruno (1548–1600).

Spanish mystics St Teresa of Avila (1515–82) and St John of the Cross (1542–91).

François de Sales (1567–1622), French Catholic mystic.

Jacob Boehme (1575–1624), Silesian Protestant mystic influenced by the Kabbala.

Caitanya, inspiration of devotional mystical movement in Hinduism.

Giordano Bruno, Italian mystic and early scientist, is tortured over a period of eight years and burnt at the stake for heresy in 1600.

1600

René Descartes (1596–1650), French mystic philosopher and mathematician.

Blaise Pascal (1623–62), French mathematician and mystic.

Angelus Silesius (1624–77), Protestant mystic and Platonist.

George Fox (1624–90), English founder of the Quakers.

Thomas Traherne (1637–74), English mystic poet and Platonist.

During the sixteenth and seventeenth centuries the Wars of Religion between Protestants and Catholics devastated Europe.

In Germany, only a third of the population remained alive. Dissatisfaction with religion gives birth to the Scientific Age.

1700

J. P. De Caussade (d. 1739), French Catholic mystic.

·William Blake (1757–1827), English mystic, poet and artist.

William Wordsworth (1770–1850), English poet and nature mystic.

Samuel Taylor Coleridge (1772–1834), English Platonist, poet and opium-taker.

1800

Alfred Lord Tennyson (1809–92), English poet and mystic.

Walt Whitman (1819–92), American transcendentalist poet.

Ramakrishna (1836–86), Hindu saint.

William James (1842–1910), American psychedelic mystic and author of *The Varieties of Religious Experience*.

Richard Jefferies (1848–87), English nature mystic.

Black Elk, Native American visionary.

Behraqmshah Shroff (1857–1927), Parsi mystic

W. B. Yeats (1865–1939), Irish mystic poet.

1900

Carl Jung (1875–1961), Swiss founding father of psychology.

Albert Einstein (1879–1955), Swiss scientist and sage.

Ramana Maharshi (1880–1949), Hindu master.

Teilhard de Chardin (1881–1955), French Jesuit priest and scientist.

Aldous Huxley (1894–1963), English psychedelic mystic and author of *The Perennial Philosophy*.

Sri Nisargadatta (1897–1981), Hindu master.

Thomas Merton (1915–68), Trappist monk.

Other great mystics of this century have included the following. Hindus: Sri Aurobindo, Radhakrishnan, Mahatma Gandhi, Neem Karoli Baba, Yogananda; Buddhists: Douglas Harding, D. T. Suzuki, Shunryu Suzuki; poets: Robert Graves, T. S. Eliot, John Lennon, Van Morrison; psychedelic mystics: Alan Watts, Timothy Leary.

Living masters include Hindus: Sai Baba, Ramesh Balsekar, Ram Dass (Richard Alpert); Buddhists: Thich Nhat Hanh, the Dalai Lama, Sogyal Rinpoche.

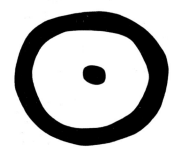

FURTHER READING

General Reading
Armstrong, K. *A History of God*, Mandarin, 1993
Balsekar, R. *Consciousness Speaks*, Zen Publications, 1992
Campbell, J. *Masks of God Series*, Arkana, 1991
Huxley, A. *The Perennial Philosophy*, Flamingo Modern Classics, 1994
Jung, C. *Memories, Dreams, Reflections*, Fontana, 1963

Shamanic Mysticism
Freke, T. and Wa'Na'Nee'Che'. *The Principles of Native American Spirituality*, Thorsons, 1996
Nicholson, S. *Shamanism*, A Quest Book, 1987

Hindu Mysticism
Dass, R. *Miracle of Love – stories about Neem Karoli Baba*, Dutton, 1979
Nisargadatta, S. *I am That*, Chetana, 1973

Buddhist Mysticism
Reps, P. *Zen Flesh, Zen Bones*, Pelican Books, 1971
Hanh, Thich Nanh, *The Sun in my Heart*, Parallax Press, 1988

Taoist Mysticism
Freke, T. *Tao Te Ching*, Piatkus, 1995

Watts, A. *Tao – The Watercourse Way*, Penguin Books, 1979

The Mystery Schools
Angus, S. *The Mystery Religions*, Dover Books, 1975
Godwin, J. *Mystery Religions in the Ancient World*, Thames and Hudson, 1981

Jewish Mysticism
Buber, M. *Jewish Mysticism*, JM Dent and Sons Ltd, 1931
Scholem, G. *Major Trends in Jewish Mysticism*, Schocken Books, 1954

Christian Mysticism
Underhill, E. *Mysticism*, One World Books, 1993
Armstrong, K. *The English Mystics of the 14th Century*, Kyle Cathie Ltd, 1991

Islamic Mysticism
Shah, I. *Tales of the Dervishes*, Panther Books, 1973
Barks, C. *Birdsong* (and all translations of Rumi), Maypop, 1993

Mysticism Outside Religion
Eliots, TS. *The Four Quartets*, Faber and Faber
Capra, F. *The Tao of Physics*, Fontana, 1976

INDEX

Page numbers in *italic* refer to the illustrations

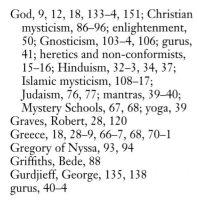

Acknowledgements

Piatkus Books would like to thank the following for their kind permission to reproduce the photographs: Barnaby's Picture Library: *Daibutsu Buddha at Kamakura; The Menorah.* The Bridgeman Art Library: *Pythagorus, from the south door of the Royal portal; School of Athens-detail Aristotle and Plato.* British Museum: *Detail of Michaelangelo's David, Jacob's Ladder.* Tim Chapman: *Mystic Eyes.* Circa Photo Library: *Taoist monk; Resurrection.* Corbis-Bettmann/UPI: *Mahatma Gandhi; Einstein; Leary in Action; Carl Jung.* Mary Evans Picture Library: *Saint Cuthbert on Farne Island; Religious Persecution; Saint Simeon the ancient, cave dweller; Buddha, Lao-tse and Confucius; Mandala.* The Hutchison Library: *Dancing Nataraja figure; Mali Dancers; 14th century fresco of Jesus Christ.* Japan Information Centre: *Monks in meditation.* Peter Sanders: *Saudi Arabia, Makkah Ka'aba; Allah in Arabic; Turkey, Whirling Dervishes.* Tibet Image Bank: *Pilgrim at Mount Kailash.* Tony Stone Images: *Fakir sitting in yoga position with feet behind head; Apache Indian Dancing, blurred motion.* Also, Faber and Faber Ltd for permission to quote from T.S. Eliot.